THINK. PLAY. ACHIEVE!

Achieve! is a research-based series for young learners. It was designed by Houghton Mifflin Harcourt, a global leader in education serving 60 million students worldwide.

WHY IS THIS BOOK DIFFERENT?

There are hundreds of opportunities to practice skills in 4 key disciplines: math, language arts, science, and social studies.

Activities are based on new educational standards that emphasize problem-solving. This leads to higher-order thinking. That's when kids take what they've learned to solve *real-life* problems, or create something new.

Activities are also nested in topics that matter to kids: animals, Mars, and fruit smoothies. Achieve! looks like a magazine, not school work. World-class photography makes pages FIZZ.

NOW SAY SOMETHING ABOUT ME!

Oh, yes. This is Cosmo. He's on hand (and he has five of them) to help.

Send all inquiries to: Permissions, The Learning Company, 222 Berkeley Street, Boston, Massachusetts, 02116-3748

ISBN: 9780544372412

www.hmhco.com

Manufactured in the United States of America

DOM 10 9 8 7 6 5 4 3 2 1

4500478018

ACHIEVE!

Edited by Sharon Emerson and Meredith Phillips

Houghton Mifflin Harcourt

Boston   New York

Contents

Reading Foundations

Unsure Bear

The bear is not sure that these words have prefixes.

Show her the prefixes. Circle them.

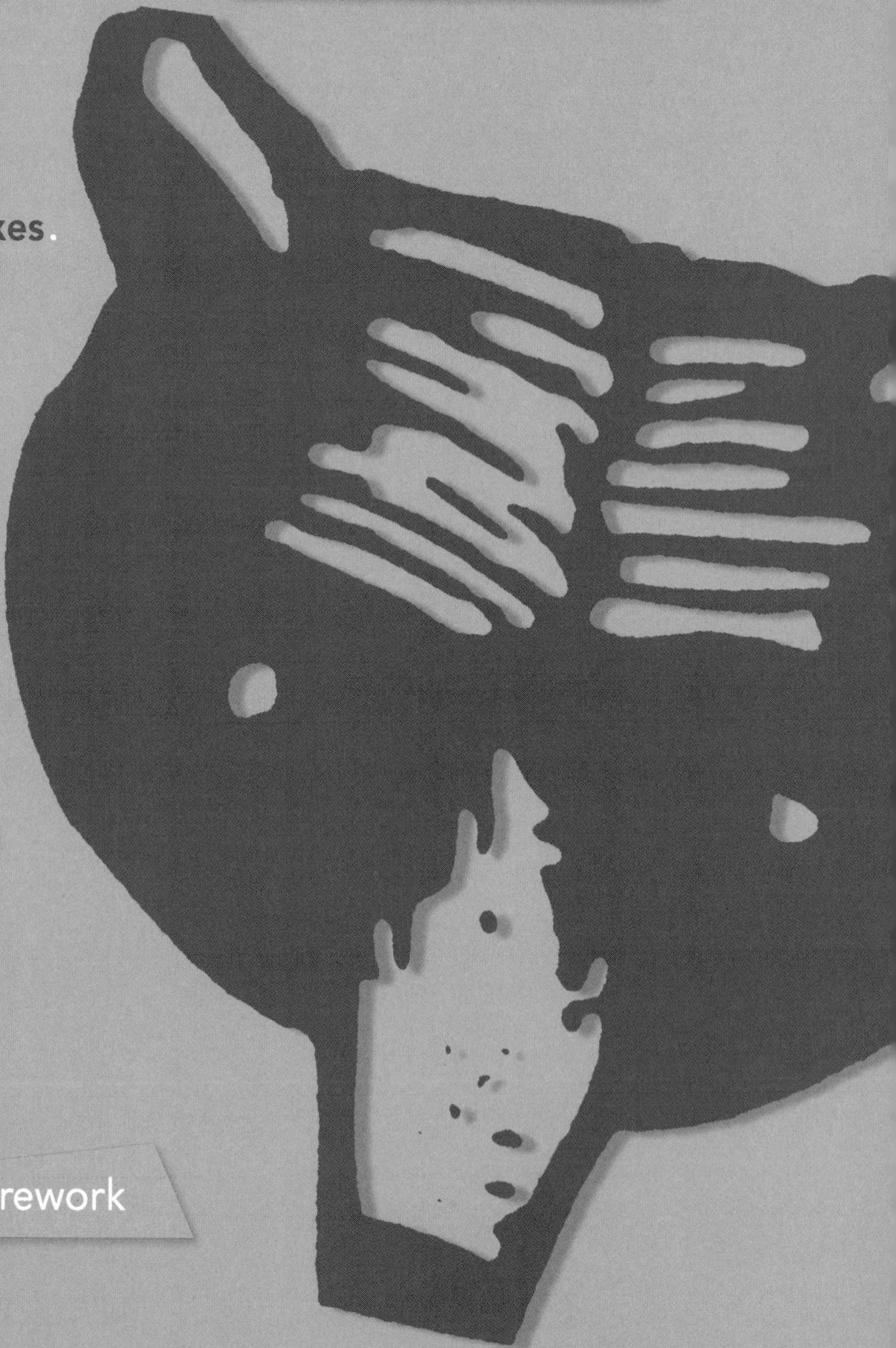

mistreat

misjudge

preview

precook

rebuild

rework

A **prefix** is a group of letters attached to the **front** of a word to make a new word. The prefix un– means *not*. Is this helpful or **un**helpful?

Let's SCRAM!

A prefix helps give a word its meaning.
Draw a line from each statement to what
the underlined prefix means.

I am <u>un</u>happy when the bear stares at me.

together

We should <u>re</u>read the scouting safety manual.

two

Can we <u>co</u>exist with the bear?

not

again

Let's hop on our <u>bi</u>cycles and get out of here!

FEED KOKO!

Koko the Komodo dragon is hungry for words. Combine **prefixes** and **roots** to make new words for Koko. Use each prefix at least once.

prefixes	
re–	bi–
un–	mis–

roots	
heat	kind
behave	cycle

_____

_____

_____

_____

Koko's plate

Undefined!

dislike _____

imperfect _____

inactive _____

invisible _____

nonfiction _____

nonliving _____

Some prefixes mean the same or similar things. The prefixes **un–**, **dis–**, **im–**, **in–**, and **non–** can all mean *not*.

Forgetful FRANCIE

Francie sent this email to Roy. She forgot the prefixes!
Add a prefix to each word.

Prefixes

im–   non–   re–   un–

New Message

To: roy@____.com

Cc:

Subject: Your visit

Hi Roy,

I cannot wait until you are here. We will have

_____stop fun! You can help me _____fill the cow

feed bins. It is safe. Be _____afraid! The cows do
not bite.

Feeling _____patient,

Francie

Spinning Sammy

Sammy spun around too fast! Now he can't spot words with **prefixes**.

Circle words that have prefixes. **Cross out words that don't.**

biscuit

misuse

ready

under

replay

bimonthly

unpack

mister

The letters *un* can be a prefix. But not in the word *uncle*. If you remove *un*, the remaining *cle* is not a familiar root word.

STILL Unsure!

The bear is doubtful that these words have suffixes.
Show her the suffixes. Circle them.

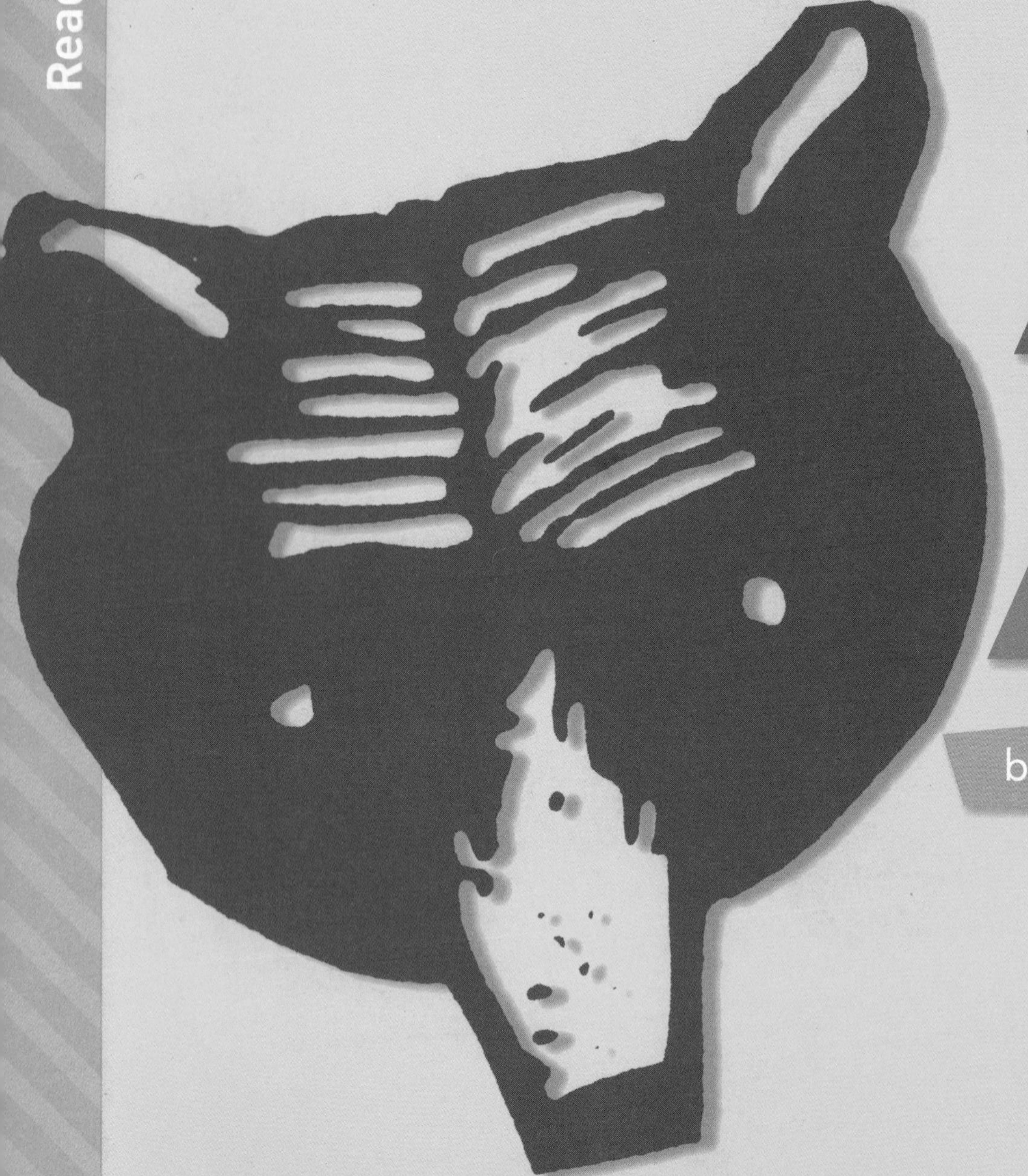

breakable

painless

powerful

windy

bravely

teacher

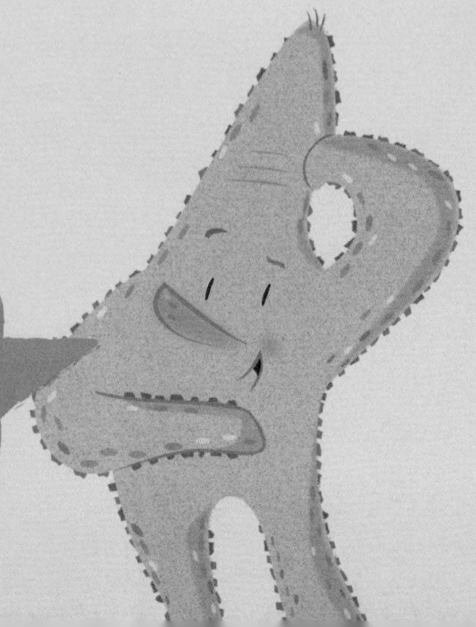

A **suffix** is a group of letters attached to the **end** of a word to make a new word. The word *careful* has a suffix. The word *terrified* does not.

A Meaningful Ending

A suffix helps give a word its meaning. **Draw a line from each statement to what the underlined** suffix means.

This chair is very comfort<u>able</u>.

I had a dream<u>less</u> night of sleep.

Jim is a skill<u>ful</u> carpenter and can make anything.

Jess is a paint<u>er</u>.

Seeing my friends gives me happi<u>ness</u>.

- one who does this
- the state of
- able to give
- full of
- without

MiXeD Messages

These signs are all wrong! Cross out wrong suffixes.
Replace them with the correct suffixes.

Suffixes

–able   –ous   –ful   –er

Our trips are adventur<u>ness</u>.

Over 50 spread<u>less</u> CHEESES!

A garden<u>ous</u> is needed to take care of plants.

Inquire within.

Try a spoon<u>ly</u> of our honey.

I made a sign. "Grace<u>ful</u> sea star gives dance less<u>ons</u>!" What would your sign say?

Blowing in the Wind!

The wind blew these words away from their definitions. **Draw a line to connect each word to its meaning.**

wind • characterized by lots of wind

windy • having no wind

windless • the movement of air

teach • to help people learn things

teacher • teach again

reteach • someone who teaches

name • having no name

nameless • what people call someone or something

misnamed • given the wrong name

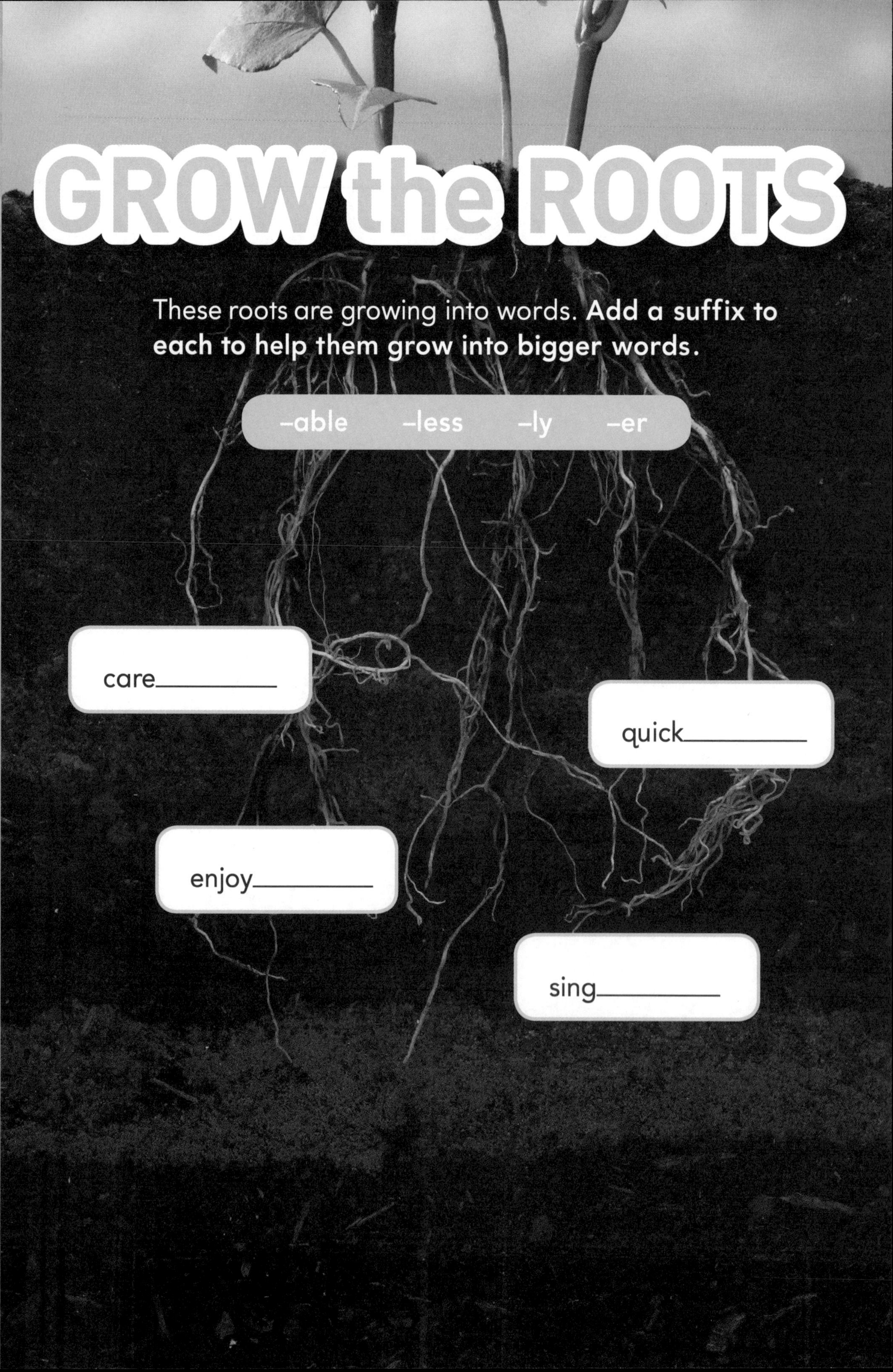

GROW the ROOTS

These roots are growing into words. **Add a suffix to each to help them grow into bigger words.**

-able   -less   -ly   -er

care_____

quick_____

enjoy_____

sing_____

THE Suffix MATRIX!

Some words can have more than one ending. Complete this matrix. Say the word with each suffix. Is it a real word? **Then make an X.**

agree	grace	friend	sick	
				–able
				–ful
				–less
				–ly
				–ness

SPELL It for OLIVE

Olive the otter sounds out words to spell them. She spelled some words wrong. **Draw a line to the** correct spelling.

Olive's spelling

agin

irth

litelee

beecuz

moov

Correct spelling

because

again

move

lightly

earth

Many words are spelled differently than how they sound. These are **irregularly spelled words**. *Sea* is an irregularly spelled word. *Star* is not.

Rules of the Road

Steer the cars into the correct tunnel.

If the word is spelled like it sounds, draw a line to the regular tunnel.

If it is spelled differently than how it sounds, draw a line to the irregular tunnel.

regular

irregular

friendly

straight

blaze

people

slump

napkin

Syl | la | ble BITES!

Sylvia likes to eat words in small bites.
Cut them up into syllables.

de | ter | mine

until

absolute

demand

consist

historic

Spelling
and
Vocabulary

Sada's Safari

Someone scrambled the signs at Sada's Safari! **Unscramble the letters to find the animals.**

latpeehn

_____

raegffi

_____

azrbe

_____

hteache

_____

oynmek

_____

oiln

_____

sitroch

_____

ilorgla

_____

A safari is a journey to look at animals. They mostly take place in Africa. To look at me, you'd need to go on a snorkel safari.

On the Menu

Sonya spilled her macchiato on the menu! She wiped it up, but now it's missing words. **Write them back in.**

Breakfast

scrambled   __ __ __ __

crispy   __ __ __ __ __

three buttermilk   __ __ __ __ __ __ __

orange   __ __ __ __ __

Macchiato (mah-kee-AH-toe) is *coffee with milk*. Which is easier to say? *You decide.*

Dinner

grilled   ___ ___ ___ ___ ___ ___ ___

mashed   ___ ___ ___ ___ ___ ___ ___ ___

green   ___ ___ ___ ___ ___

skim   ___ ___ ___ ___

HAPPY, Not Sad!

Complete each set of **antonyms**. Then use the antonym you wrote to fill in the word puzzle.

Down

1. safe, not _____

2. tall, not _____

4. wide, not _____

Across

3. boring, not _____

5. entrance, not _____

6. up, not _____

Antonyms are words that mean the opposite of each other, like *soft* and *hard*. *Salty* and *fresh*.

IT'S A PAIR

Synonyms

cheap   clap   dirty   leap   quiet   smart

silent

_____

filthy

_____

inexpensive

_____

jump

_____

intelligent

_____

applaud

_____

Synonyms are words that have similar meanings, like *pink* and *fuchsia*.

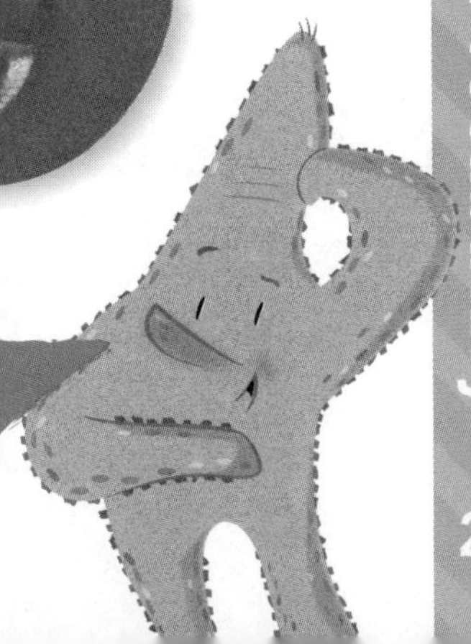

TERRIBLE Termites!

Two termites ate through these words. **Write the missing letters.**

cr ___ ___ d

l ___ ___ n

cl ___ ___ d

ch ___ ___ k

___ ___ een

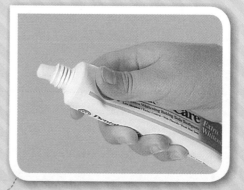

s ___ ___ eeze

HELP HARRY!

Where is Ernie?

Harry the hedgehog always gets lost. Add **scr** to the letters in each column. If it makes a word, circle it. **Make a path to Ernie!**

__ __ __ z	__ __ __ c	__ __ __ sh	__ __ __ am
__ __ __ ed	__ __ __ any	__ __ __ tch	__ __ __ ape
__ __ __ om	__ __ __ ifle	__ __ __ eam	__ __ __ ou
__ __ ness	__ __ __ atch	__ __ __ ils	__ __ __ dge
__ __ __ ub	__ __ __ ip	__ __ __ ble	__ __ __ se

Where is Harry? Dinner is cold.

Find It!

Complete each sentence. Then find the words in the puzzle.

apple	ladder	summer	uncle	whistle	winter

I have one _____ but no aunts.

You can climb a _____.

He likes to eat an _____ a day.

The coldest season of the year is _____.

The hottest season of the year is _____.

Blowing on a _____ makes a loud noise.

```
u n c l e t j z r n
e l t s i h w e r d
m x j u l n m r f m
r f a r q m g e l s
p e m t u z i t t z
q p d s a n d n b g
c y b d v p r i k j
j a v c a m p w c u
u q d d l l w l a z
z n o f w g m j e z
```

Seeing Double

These crazy glasses make you see double!
Make an **X** over words that have too many letters.
Then circle words that are spelled correctly.

sudden

dessign

chappter

lesson

letter

pillow

happen

incclude

All in a DAY

You are not going to believe this...

Terry the toad had an interesting day. Complete the story to find out what happened to him. Write the correct spelling of each word.

_____, I was hopping through the forest when I heard a

(Todai/Today)

_____. I looked up and saw a boy walking on the

(noise/noyse)

_____. The boy was wearing a crown of _____ and a

(trail/trayl)   (goald/gold)

purple cape. At first, I thought it was a _____, but he was

(dream/dreem)

_____. I was looking at a prince! I hopped home and

(real/reel)

_____ all of the toads I could find!

(told/towld)

Some **vowel sounds** can be spelled different ways. The *long e* sound can be spelled *e_e, ee* or *ea*. Which way is it spelled in sea star?

Story Time

Make up a story. Use the pictures shown in your story.

What's on Your Brain Mind, Marty?

Marty the mole will tell you everything—but he does not choose his words carefully. Help him to be clearer. **Replace the underlined word with a better word.**

I do not like it when people <u>glance</u> at me for more than one minute. **(look/stare)**

I <u>nibble</u> my food quickly when I am very hungry. **(eat/gobble)**

I prefer mild, <u>scorching</u> days when the sun does not blaze down on me. **(warm/hot)**

I am <u>content</u> with my life and it could not be better! **(happy/elated)**

Now use two of the words you replaced to tell about yourself.

_____

_____

_____

You Ought to Know

Use **augh** or **ough** to complete each word.
Then say the word.

If the gh makes an *f* sound, draw a line from
the word to the trough.

r __ __ __ __

c __ __ __ __ t

th __ __ __ __ t

l __ __ __ __

t __ __ __ __

br __ __ __ __ t

d __ __ __ __ ter

Translate It!

Nico is visiting from the Alps. He does not understand some of our idioms.

Draw a line to match each saying to what it means.

Idiom

They are a dime a dozen.

That will be a piece of cake.

It's a toss-up.

We're all in the same boat.

Meaning

That will be easy.

We all have the same problem.

They are not very special.

It could go either way.

An **idiom** has a different meaning than what the words mean. When you are talking, *I am all ears!* That means, *I am listening!* Clearly, I am all arms.

Now explain these idioms to Nico. **Write what they mean.**

It's raining cats and dogs.

_____

_____

_____

You are the apple of my eye.

_____

_____

_____

Actions speak louder than words.

_____

_____

_____

Drop It, Edie!

Edie the eel forgot to drop the **e** before adding **–ed** or **–ing**. Write the correct spelling of each word.

inviteed

_____

changeing

_____

tasteed

_____

saveing

_____

stareed

_____

jokeing

_____

CHANGE IT, YAN!

Yikes! Yan the yak won't let go of his y's. **Correct the words he wrote.**

Change the y to i before adding –es or –ed.

cryed

_____

puppyes

_____

cityes

_____

tryed

_____

Now circle the words that are plurals. Box the words that show the past tense.

carryed

_____

partyes

_____

DR. Dictionary

Label the parts of this dictionary entry.

_____   _____

hes·i·tate hez-ə-tate, verb

hesitates; hesitated; hesitating

to stop briefly before doing
something.

*Tom hesitated before jumping into
the lake.*

_____   _____

_____

Labels

definition

example sentence

inflected forms

part of speech

pronunciation

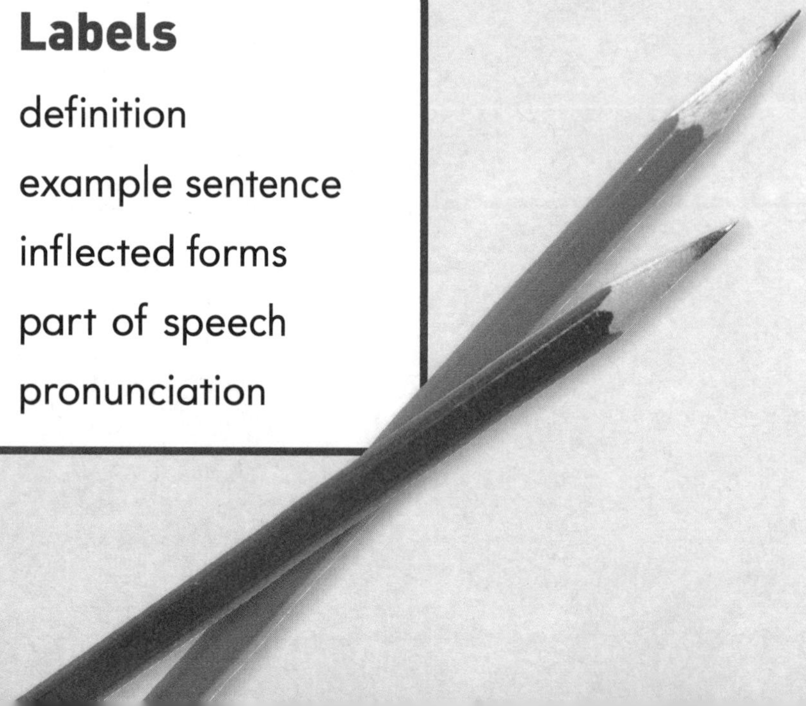

Words with endings are hard to find in the dictionary.
Write the word you would look for instead.

gliding _____ *glide* _____

wished _____

softer _____

hurried _____

understandable _____

What is your favorite word? Write a dictionary entry for it.

I enjoy using a **thesaurus**. It's like a dictionary for synonyms. A synonym for *hesitate* is *dilly-dally*.

YIP! YIP!

These dogs look different, but they sound the same!
The same is true of some words. Write the correct
homophones under each set of pictures.

beet

flour

hare

flower

beat

hair

_____

_____

_____

_____

_____

_____

Does Not BELONG?

Each **homograph** has a definition that does not belong to it. Cross it out.

park

to stop a car in a certain place

relating to your health

a place with grass to play

bat

a tool used in baseball

an area around a lake

a type of animal

change

to make something different

letter

a message mailed to someone

feeling very happy

a bunch of coins

the top of a building

a symbol in the alphabet

The word *star* is a **homograph**. It can be a *fiery object in outer space*. Or it can be a *fiery little echinoderm*, like me!

Spelling and Vocabulary

Hurry, Paco!

Paco likes to go fast! Write **contractions** to show Paco how to say these words *faster*.

have not _____

does not _____

are not _____

could not _____

he is _____

there is _____

what is _____

she is _____

SPEED
LIMIT
PACO

A **contraction** is one or more shortened words. The apostrophe stands for the letters that are left out, like the "o" in isn't.

Grammar
and
Mechanics

Noun Jar

A burglar stole some nouns and hid them in a cookie jar. **Find the nouns. Circle them.**

happy

bring

walk

family

table

quickly

dry

difficult

car

room

dog

sky

NOUNS

Now the burglar has hidden proper nouns in the jar. **Find and circle them.**

Sparky

school

woman

park

Mrs. Jones

White House

Central Park

dog

structure

Eiffel Tower

building

Banfield School

A **noun** names a person, animal, place, or thing, like a *burglar*. A **proper noun** names a specific person, animal, place, or thing, like *Sam* the burglar.

Pack It Right!

Help Joey pack for a trip. Write the **concrete nouns** in her suitcase. Write the **abstract nouns** in her thought bubble.

book   comb   friendship   hope   joy

_____

_____

_____

_____

shirt   soap   strength

A **concrete noun** names something you can see and touch. An **abstract noun** names an idea or feeling. I see you looking at my **bucket** of popcorn. My **hope** is that you won't touch it.

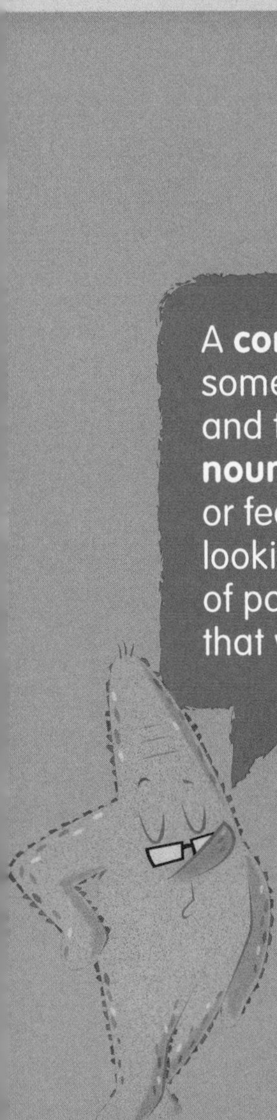

Garage Sale

Robbie labeled these items for the sale.
But there is more than one of each item.

Fix the labels. Make each noun **plural**.

two coat

_____

two tray

_____

four plate

_____

three dress

_____

three ruby

_____

Garage SALE!

Add –s or –es to most nouns to make them **plural**. If the word ends in y, ask yourself if it rhymes with e like he. If it does, change the y to i before adding –es.

These nouns are **irregular**. Fix the plurals.

three loafs

_____

three mouses

_____

two knifes

_____

four oxes

_____

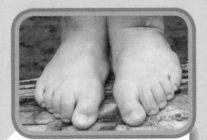

two foots

_____

Giraffe is a **regular** noun. Just add an *–s* to make it plural. *Giraffes. Calf* is **irregular**. Change the *f* to *ve*. Then add *–s* to make it plural. *Calves.* The *giraffes* have baby cal*ves*.

On the Right Path

Write each verb on its correct path.

waited	will wait	waits
starts	started	will start
will bake	bakes	baked

Past Tense

_____

_____

_____

Present Tense

_____

_____

_____

Future Tense

_____

_____

_____

A **present tense** action is happening now. A **past tense** action happened in the past. It usually ends in *–ed*. A **future tense** action *will* happen in the future.

Yesterday

Jaden did many things yesterday. Write the **past tense** form of each verb. Then find it in the puzzle. (It may be backwards, diagonal, or both!)

allow _____

cook _____

need _____

like _____

pretend _____

trade _____

If the verb ends in *e*, then drop the *e* and add *–ed* to make it past tense.

J V M A Y O N W G C
D M X W G E R G O O
P R E T E N D E D O
A M M D O U P R H K
Q L E D W T W Q Y E
N D L D E D A R T D
T Y P O W K Y Y E X
Y T K H W Q I J U U
N T T C J E G L K X
V L K H N Y D E G J

Password
From the Past

The password to this tree house changes every day. Circle the correct verb in each sentence. That's the password of the day!

SUNDAY: He (saw/seen) the movie last week.

MONDAY: They (gone/went) into the restaurant.

TUESDAY: I (did/done) that yesterday.

WEDNESDAY: She has (ran/run) indoors many times.

THURSDAY: He had (gone/went) to sleep by the time we got there.

FRIDAY: I have (saw/seen) a horse in that barn.

SATURDAY: They have (did/done) that before.

The verbs *come, do, go, run,* and *see* are **irregular**. I *did* not see that coming!

A "Be" for Bob

Beetle Bob thinks **be** is the perfect verb. But most times, another form of **be** is needed.
Circle the correct form of **be** for each sentence.

She (am/was) happy after the meeting.

Our car (is/were) red.

I (am/is) ready to sing in the show.

The leaves (was/were) colorful last fall.

They (are/is) teachers at our school.

Complete the chart to show Bob when to use the different forms of **be**.

	Present Tense	Past Tense
I	am	
He, She, It		was
You		were
They	are	
We	are	

The verb **be** describes a state of existence. It can be a long-term state, such as *I am a sea star!* It can also be a short-term state, such as *I was tired after my long swim.*

State It Simply—Or Not

Draw a line from each **sentence type** to an **example**.

Sentence type	Example

A **simple sentence** tells one complete thought.

● Even though it was raining, we went outside.

A **compound sentence** is made up of two simple sentences joined by *am*, *but*, *or*, or *so*.

● We went outside.

A **complex sentence** is made up of an independent clause and a dependent clause.

● We went outside, and we played in the rain.

Circle **subjects** in the example sentences above. Then underline the **verbs**.

An **independent clause** tells a complete thought. *I like chips.* A **dependent clause** does not. It sounds unfinished! *When I wear a hat.*

Too Little, Too Much

Mindy the mouse speaks in nibbles. Change her sentence fragments into complete sentences. **Add a subject to these fragments.**

plays soccer. _____

helped the teacher. _____

Add a verb to these fragments.

She one book that week. _____

Tom the ball to Sally. _____

Unlike Mindy, George the giraffe goes on at length. Fix his run-on sentences. **Rewrite them as a compound sentence or as two sentences.**

Mitch likes to read mysteries his favorite food is toast.

_____

_____

The store is open every day they sell candles and soap.

_____

_____

Down to Earth

Flor just arrived from Planet Phos-5.
Show her how we communicate.
Draw a line from each sentence type **to an** example.

Sentence type	Example
A **statement** tells something.	You have a strong handshake!
A **question** asks something. It ends with a question mark.	Stay on Earth, please.
A **command** tells someone to do something.	You traveled a long way.
An **exclamation** shows strong feeling. It ends with an exclamation point.	Are you from outer space?

Flor shows you a photo of her home. **Write four sentences to respond to it.**

Statement: _____

_____

Question: _____

_____

Command: _____

_____

Exclamation: _____

_____

Now show Flor how **subjects** and **verbs** must agree.
Circle the correct verb in each sentence.

The people of Earth (is/are) happy to greet you!

We (hope/hopes) you enjoy your stay on Earth.

When you (visit/visits) Florida, wear sunscreen.

Will any of your siblings (join/joins) you on this trip?

I (want/wants) to visit your planet.

So (do/does) my brother.

Ask your parents if we can (return/returns) home with you.

ANTECEDENT HUNT!

Henry the hound smells an **antecedent**. Join the hunt.
Draw a line from the bolded pronoun to its antecedent.

Olivia wanted to read the book because **it** was a mystery.

Joe kicked the ball into the goal
and everyone congratulated **him**.

Logan called **his** grandmother every weekend.

Now write the correct pronoun to match
its antecedent.

Ms. Heath said that _____ would
feed our dog while we were away.

My friends thought _____ saw me
at the store yesterday.

The movie got bad reviews, so no
one wanted to see _____ .

The **antecedent** usually comes before the pronoun, as
shown above. But sometimes it comes after. *After* **she**
ate, **my sister** *waited one hour before swimming.*

ME, MYSELF, and SCHOOL

Complete these sentences to tell about yourself.
Circle the correct **pronoun**.

My _____ wakes (I/me) up for school.

(I/Me) like to arrive at school _____.

Sometimes my teacher asks (I/me) to _____.

(I/Me) always say, "_____!"

At lunchtime, (I/me) eat with _____.

After, my friends and (I/me) play _____.

The bell rings. It's time for (I/me) to _____!

Draw a picture of something you like to do after school.

Use the pronoun **I** or **me** in a sentence to tell what you are doing.

_____

_____

MINE.

Patty the pack rat thinks everything belongs to her. Show her that some things are not, in fact, hers. **Write the possessive form of each noun.**

Her sister _'s_ hairbrush

Luke ＿＿ hat

The babies ＿＿ bottles

The children ＿＿ toys

The flower＿＿ petals

The school ＿＿ chalk

The men ＿＿ bowties

The chickens ＿＿ coop

Iowa ＿＿ flag

Show who owns it! Most of the time, add an *apostrophe* and *s*. *I borrowed James's shoes.* But if the noun is plural and ends in an *s*, then only add the *apostrophe. The shoes' laces were broken!*

Show Patty that pronouns can be possessive, too.
Circle the correct possessive form of each pronoun.
Cross out the incorrect form.

I → I's
mine

you → yours
you's

he → him
his

she → her
hers

we → we's
ours

they → them's
theirs

it → it's
its

Finish these sentences.

The _____ belongs to _____.

It is _____!
    (possessive pronoun)

LOOK CLOSELY

Some pronouns are **homophones**. They sound the same, but mean different things. **Circle the correct homophone for each sentence.**

Let's take (your/you're) dog for a walk.

(Its/It's) a nice day today.

They will be happy when (their/they're) home again.

If (your/you're) tired, you should go to sleep.

Put the toy back in (its/it's) box.

(Their/They're) house is two blocks from ours.

If you're unsure, read the contraction as two words. *You're* is the same as *you are*. *It's* is the same as *it is*. *They're* is the same as *they are*.

UP the MOUNTAIN

Complete these sentences to tell about the picture. Choose from the words below.

down   near   safely   slowly   yesterday

Carla and her dad arrived _____.

They climbed _____.

After many hours, they reached the top _____.

They set up camp _____ a stream.

The next morning, they started _____ the mountain.

Draw a ⭐ over the adverb that tells *when* something happened.

Circle adverbs that tell *where* something happened.

Box adverbs that tell *how* something happened.

Treasure Finder

You joined an archaeological *(ar-kee-uh-loj-i-kuhl)* dig. You found fantastic treasures. Describe them in your journal. Circle the correct **adjective**.

Slurp!
I found two tea servers. The one on the left is (smaller/smallest) than the one on the right.

I found three musical instruments. The one on the right is the (larger/largest) in the group.

An **adjective** describes a noun. Cute, cuter, and cutest are **adjectives**. These are three ways to describe a sea star.

Complete your journal entries. Circle the correct **adverb**.

I found two calendars. The one on the left is (more/most) modern.

On the final day, I found a spoon, a lantern, and a statue. The (more/most) interesting artifact is the _____.

An **adverb** can describe an adjective. I am *more* interesting than my cousin Gareth. I might be the *most* interesting echinoderm in the world! (I'm still asking around.)

KEEP it SHORT

Write the **abbreviation** for underlined days, months, and places.

My week at a glance

Monday

[ ] Dentist on Lincoln Street [ ]

Tuesday

[ ]

Wednesday

[ ] Visit Grandma on Ocean Road [ ]

Thursday

[ ] Last day of November! [ ]

Friday

[ ] Hello, December! [ ]

Saturday

[ ]

Sunday

[ ] Block party on Jones Avenue [ ]

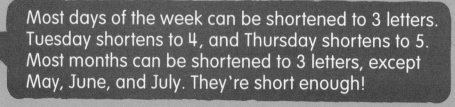

Most days of the week can be shortened to 3 letters. Tuesday shortens to 4, and Thursday shortens to 5. Most months can be shortened to 3 letters, except May, June, and July. They're short enough!

A Long, Long, Long Time Warp Ago

You traveled back in time. *To a classroom!*
Show the children how commas are used in the future.
Add commas below.

Eddie Bart and Ava went to the park.

We need to buy apples bananas and oranges at the store.

My dog likes to walk sleep and play.

The audience listened laughed and clapped during the play.

The children seem happy, excited, and a little nervous to see you. Maybe it's time to travel back to the future. Turn the page!

Get Into It !

Carmen wants to write a great American novel. She tries to write the perfect first sentence.

Circle the preposition in each sentence.

> The path goes around the lake.
>
> The flowers will bloom in the summer.
>
> We skied down the mountain.
>
> The book belongs on that shelf.

Now underline the prepositional phrase in each sentence.

> My cousin lives in the city.
>
> The children played on the monkey bars.
>
> We will eat at noon.
>
> I see a storm brewing in the distance.

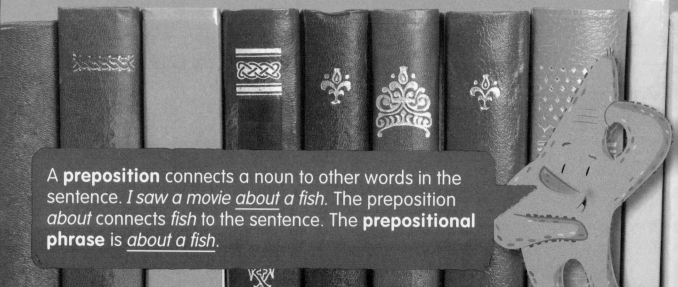

A **preposition** connects a noun to other words in the sentence. *I saw a movie about a fish.* The preposition *about* connects *fish* to the sentence. The **prepositional phrase** is *about a fish*.

Reading

Living Things

A Retelling of an African Tale

by Dina McClellan

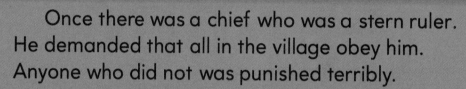

Once there was a chief who was a stern ruler. He demanded that all in the village obey him. Anyone who did not was punished terribly.

Only one person was not afraid of the chief. That was his grandmother. Who knows why the chief did not punish her. Maybe he just didn't take notice of her.

Underline two sentences that help you determine the meaning of *stern.*

Circle a *stern* look.

What is another word for *stern*? _____

74

Are Linked

One night the chief couldn't sleep. The frogs outside were making too much noise. This was a serious problem for the chief.

He woke up all the people in the village. "If I can't sleep, no one will sleep," he said. "Kill all the frogs!"

Underline the sentence that tells why the chief couldn't sleep.

Circle the sentence that tells the chief's solution for this problem.

The chief is described as *stern*. Write two of your own words to describe him.

_____   _____

So the people killed all the frogs. Later they felt ashamed. They did not like what they had done. They were all afraid of the chief.

Only the chief's grandmother was not afraid. "You'll be sorry," she said. "All living things are linked. Even you and the frogs."

The chief had to laugh. "How could frogs be linked to a big chief like me?" he said.

Underline one sentence that helps you understand why the people felt *ashamed*.

Circle an *ashamed* look.

What is another word for *ashamed*? _____

An ashamed person feels shame.

Soon it was time for the harvest. Everyone in the village had to gather beans and sweet potatoes. It was hard to work outdoors. The air was full of mosquitoes. Thousands of them!

The chief stayed in his hut while others worked. The mosquitoes found him there. He couldn't sleep or think. There was too much buzzing! The chief was covered with bites.

Underline two details that show this is a worse problem than the frogs.

Draw a picture of the chief suffering from his new problem.

"Kill the mosquitoes!" the chief said. "I want every last one killed by the morning!"

"Why didn't you take my advice?" said the grandmother. "We are in this mess because you killed the frogs."

The chief paid no attention to her. Again he told the villagers to kill the mosquitoes.

Imagine you are a villager.
What would you say to the chief?

Write your words in the speech bubble.

Kill the mosquitoes!

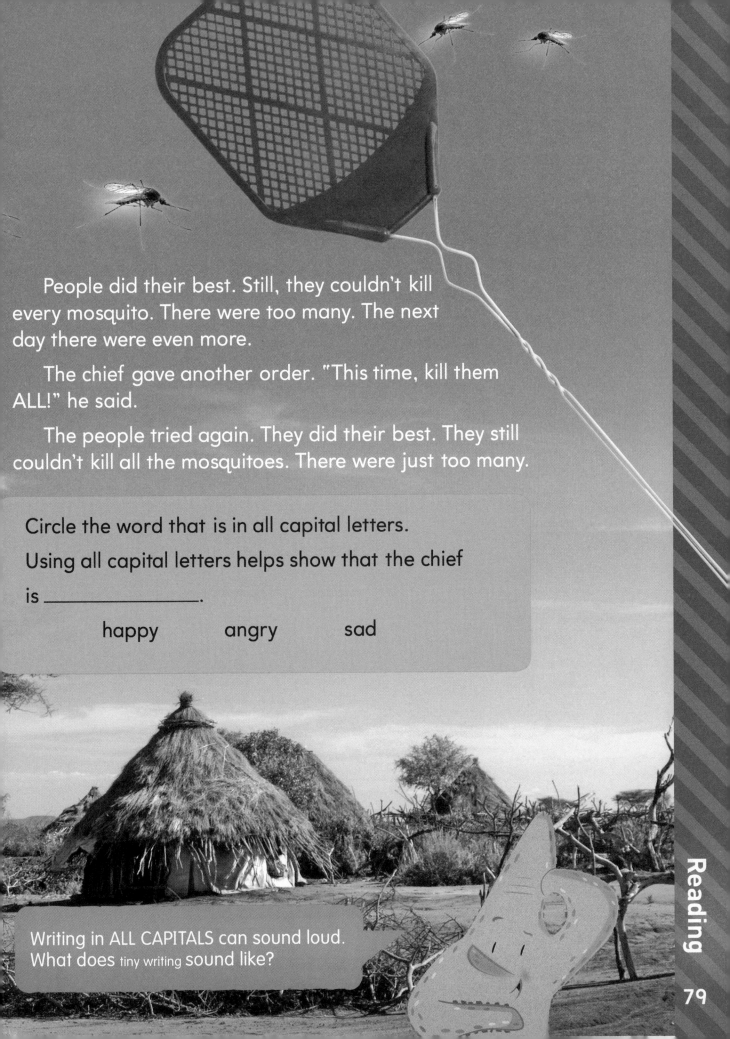

People did their best. Still, they couldn't kill every mosquito. There were too many. The next day there were even more.

The chief gave another order. "This time, kill them ALL!" he said.

The people tried again. They did their best. They still couldn't kill all the mosquitoes. There were just too many.

Circle the word that is in all capital letters.

Using all capital letters helps show that the chief is _____.

happy   angry   sad

Writing in ALL CAPITALS can sound loud.
What does tiny writing sound like?

You should have left those frogs alone," said the grandmother.

"What are you talking about?" said the chief. He was very angry.

"Don't you know that frogs eat mosquitoes? That's why you need frogs!" the grandmother said.

At last, the chief learned his lesson. He found out the hard way that all living things are linked.

Draw a line to complete the moral of the story.

the villagers must work outdoors.

Respect nature because   all living things are linked.

frogs face many dangers.

Circle the paragraph that gives one example of how living things are linked.

A **moral** is the big idea or message of the story.

A chief in a neighboring village is also complaining about the frogs.

Advise the chief. Tell him what to do. Tell him what not to do.

Are the frogs too loud? Try doing this:

_____

_____

Do not do this:

_____

_____

Draw two living things that are linked.

Many animals eat mosquitoes, including bats, birds, and dragonflies. But the mosquitofish may like them best!

Sprinting JOYCE

by Mia Lewis

Joyce had a big brother. His name was Roy. He drove her to school each day. When they arrived, he always said the same thing.

"See you later, slowpoke!"

This was starting to bug Joyce. She had joined the track team. Her coach didn't think she was a slowpoke!

Underline the sentence that tells what Roy says to Joyce.

Circle the word in the sentence that bugs Joyce.

Draw a picture of Joyce after Roy says this to her. Show how it makes her feel.

Joyce told her friend Leslie what was going on.

"Roy is the sports editor of the school paper," said Leslie. "I'll write some articles about the team. I'll give you a nickname. I'll say you are a great athlete. Roy won't know it's you. Once he finds out, he'll know you aren't a slowpoke."

Joyce smiled. "This sounds like fun!"

Underline three words that describe Joyce's friend Leslie.

loyal   helpful   uncaring

bossy   clever   mean

Roy thinks Joyce is a slowpoke. How could Leslie's plan change his mind?

_____

_____

I love it when a plan comes together!

Leslie told her plan to the track team.

"From now on," she said, "Joyce will be SJ. It stands for Sprinting Joyce. Don't tell Roy!"

"Your secret is safe!" said Meg and Rita.

"You just have to run fast, Joyce!" said Leslie. "Then our plan will succeed.

"I'll try!" said Joyce.

Who knows about Leslie's plan?

Write the names in the correct box.

Knows About It	Does Not Know About It

Why does Leslie tell them about the plan?

_____

_____

What nickname would you give to a fast runner?

_____

My cousin's name is Gareth.
But I call him "The Hedgehog."
That's his nickname.

SJ Makes Team

by Leslie Chin

What's the buzz around school? It's about our girls' track team. They are fast, and they keep winning. They may even earn a spot at the state track meet!

The rising star is SJ. This sprinter is no slowpoke! She can contribute more speed to the team. SJ will help them win.

Circle the word in the first paragraph that is an antonym for *slow*.

Why does Leslie use words like *fast*, *speed*, *star*, and *win* in her article?

_____

_____

_____

Some people think I'm a slowpoke. It can take me one minute to move six inches. Compared to a paper clip, I'd say that's pretty fast.

"Now I have to win!" said Joyce.

"Don't worry," said Leslie. "Just don't tell Roy how fast you run. He'll be so surprised!"

Just then, Roy walked by their table. "Who is this SJ?" he asked.

"You must be kidding!" Meg said. "Everybody knows SJ!"

Did Roy read Leslie's article?   Yes ☐   No ☐

Underline the sentence that helps you know whether he read it.

What do you think Roy will say when he learns that Joyce is SJ?

Write down two lines of dialogue for him.

"_____

_____!" Roy said.

"_____

_____," he said.

Use quotation marks to show what someone says out loud.

"I wish I could tell Roy," said Joyce. "He thinks I'm warming the bench."

"Just run," said Leslie.

Track Coach Predicts Victory

by Leslie Chin

Get set for a big win! Our girls' track team is filled with excitement. SJ is heating up the track. We're all rooting for her!

The coach is happy, too! "I think SJ will take us to the top," she said.

Draw a line to match the idioms from the story to their meanings.

heating up the track   help us win

take us to the top   not running in the race

warming the bench   running really fast

Write another line of dialogue for Joyce to end the page. Use one of these idioms:

- will be a piece of cake (will be easy)

- a toss up (could go either way)

- bitten off more than I can chew (taken on a task that is too hard for me)

- cross your fingers (hope good things for me)

"_____

_____!" Joyce said.

It was time for their next race. Joyce led the team to a big win.

"Did you know that SJ is short for Sprinting Joyce?" Leslie asked Roy.

Roy smiled. "I won't call you slowpoke anymore," he said. "I promise!"

Joyce was happy. Leslie wrote about the race. She chose a headline for her story: "Winning Team Gets Cheers from Roy!"

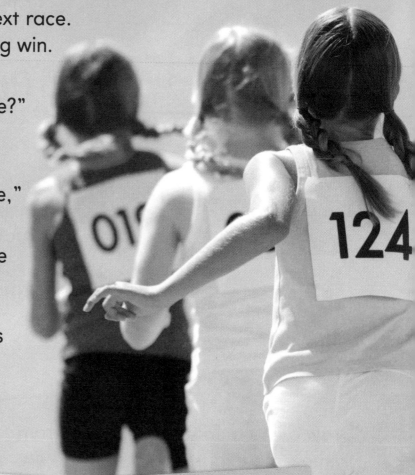

Check the box that best describes how Roy feels.

☐ proud   ☐ angry   ☐ embarrassed   ☐ sad

Underline the detail that helps you understand how Roy feels.

Draw a picture showing how Roy feels when Leslie tells him that SJ is Joyce.

You are a reporter, just like Leslie.

Plan an article telling about Joyce's problem and solution. Complete the chart.

Joyce's Problem
Her brother Roy calls her _____.

↓

First Step to Solving Problem
Leslie writes an article about _____ saying that she is a _____ runner, but says her name is _____.

↓

Second Step to Solving Problem
Joyce leads the team to a big _____.

↓

Solution
Roy realizes that Joyce is a _____ runner, and says that he will no longer call her_____.

Compare the stories. Make an X if the detail describes the story.

	Living Things Are Linked	Sprinting Joyce
problem is solved		
problem is not solved		
a character learns a lesson		

Aleck's Big Ideas

by Candyce Norvell

Inventions and Inventors

Think of great inventions of the last one hundred years. The telephone, television, car, and computer are a few of them.

We know how amazing these things are. What about the people who made them? An inventor can be as amazing as his or her invention. This is the story of one amazing inventor.

Underline the sentence that tells the topic of this text.

Now draw a picture of your favorite invention.

How does it make your life better?

_____

A **topic** is what the text is about. It can show up at the beginning or end of the introduction. Off-topic, that is an amazing shirt you are wearing!

A Boy Named Aleck

In 1847, a boy named Aleck was born in Scotland. He became interested in sound.

One day Aleck got lost. He heard his father calling him from far away. This made Aleck curious about how sound traveled.

As a joke, Aleck and his brothers made a machine. It sounded like a baby crying. Their neighbors thought it was a real baby!

Aleck was born in Edinburgh, Scotland.

Fill in the missing effect.

Aleck heard his father calling him from far away.	→	

Fill in the missing cause.

	→	The neighbors thought they heard a baby crying.

Let's play a **cause** and **effect** game. Finish the sentence. If *it is my birthday,* then _____. (I hope you say *there will be clownfish!*)

Early Experiences

Aleck tried new experiments. He even taught his dog to talk! He rubbed its voice box. He moved its jaws. The sounds that came out were like words. Soon the dog could say, "How are you, grandmamma?"

When Aleck was 14, he made a useful machine. Until then, farmers had to take the shell off wheat. Only then could people eat it. The young genius made a machine that did this job.

How are you, grandmamma?

Write **true** or **false** for each statement.

- Aleck taught his dog to talk by singing to it. _____

- Aleck built a machine for farmers. _____

- The machine chopped wheat in half. _____

The author calls Aleck a genius. How would you describe Aleck?

Aleck is _____ and _____.

Growing Up

Aleck's mother was deaf. Aleck wanted to help her understand the things he said. He wanted to help people who could not hear well.

Aleck went to England to study. He met scientists there. He learned about a new idea called electricity.

Cross out the subhead on this section. Write a new subhead next to it.

Now complete the caption for this photograph.

Aleck's mother, Eliza Grace Bell was _____, which inspired him to _____.

A **subhead** is usually a word or phrase. It tells the reader what a section is about.

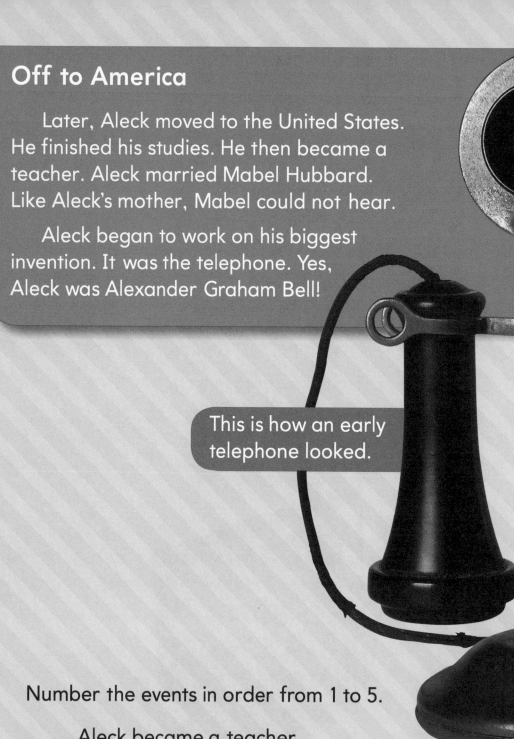

Off to America

Later, Aleck moved to the United States. He finished his studies. He then became a teacher. Aleck married Mabel Hubbard. Like Aleck's mother, Mabel could not hear.

Aleck began to work on his biggest invention. It was the telephone. Yes, Aleck was Alexander Graham Bell!

This is how an early telephone looked.

Number the events in order from 1 to 5.

_____ Aleck became a teacher.

_____ Aleck began working on his biggest invention.

_____ Aleck married Mabel Hubbard.

_____ Aleck finished his studies.

_____ Aleck moved to the United States.

Sending a Message

Aleck had an idea. He wanted to send voice messages over a wire. He and his friend Tom Watson began to try. They worked long hours in their laboratory.

During one experiment, Aleck hurt himself. Tom was in another room. Aleck said, "Mr. Watson, come here." Tom heard Aleck's voice over the wire! The first telephone message had been sent.

Aleck spoke into the transmitter. Tom heard Aleck's voice over the receiver.

What did Aleck say?
Fill in the speech bubble.

Draw a line from the picture to the paragraph it describes.

Circle some ways we communicate today.

A picture can help readers understand what they are reading.

Other Inventions

Aleck made many inventions. He made an air conditioner, a metal detector, and other useful machines.

Alexander Graham Bell once said, "All really big discoveries are the results of thought." Aleck must have thought a lot. He made some very big discoveries! Every day, other people's thoughts lead to discoveries, too.

Alexander Graham Bell invented many useful machines.

Write down two words or phrases the author uses that shows she has a positive opinion of Alexander Graham Bell.

_____   _____

Why do you think the author wrote this text?

_____

_____

A **biography** tells about someone's life. Who would you write a biography about?

Fig. 1.

An invention can use an earlier invention, as long as it does something new.

What earlier invention did the inventor use?

_____

What new thing does the invention do?

_____

What name would you give this invention?

_____

Now draw your own invention. Then tell how it helps people.

_____

_____

PUPPETS
Around the World

by Lois Grippo

People love puppets! They are a familiar toy. Children all around the world love to play with them.

Shadow Puppets

Long ago, people in Southeast Asia made shadow puppets. These puppets were flat. They were made from paper. The puppet was attached to a stick. Moving the stick made the puppet move.

The puppets were held behind a silk screen. Candles were lit to make shadows. People sat on the other side of the screen. They saw large puppet shadows on the silk screen!

> The audience only sees the puppet's shadow.

Circle the name of the type of puppet described in this section. Underline where this type of puppet was made.

Complete the sentences:

The audience did not see the _____.

Instead, they saw the puppet's _____.

> This text is called **informational text**. It gives information about a topic.

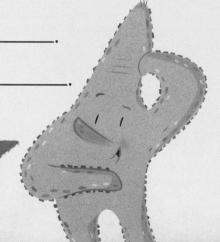

Bunraku Puppets

People in other parts of Asia also make special puppets. People in Japan make Bunraku puppets. These puppets are large. They can be as a big as a person.

It takes three people to move these puppets. The people appear on stage with the puppet.

The puppet's movements are never jerky. People work hard to make the puppets move smoothly.

Underline the word that means the opposite of *jerky* in the last paragraph.

Write a definition for *jerky*.

_____

_____

Which is *jerky*? Circle it.

Swings

Bumper cars

Hand Puppets

Did you ever make a sock puppet? A sock puppet is a hand puppet.

There were hand puppets long ago in China. These puppets were not made from socks. They were made from wood. The wood was hollow. A person's hand fit inside.

The sock puppet is a modern day version of the ancient Chinese hand puppet.

Draw a line from the puppet to two details about it.

shadow puppet

can be made from socks

can be made from wood

Bunraku puppet

made from paper

attached to a stick

hand puppet

as big as a person

moves smoothly

You can use your hands to make shadow puppets.
Match the hand shape to the shadow.

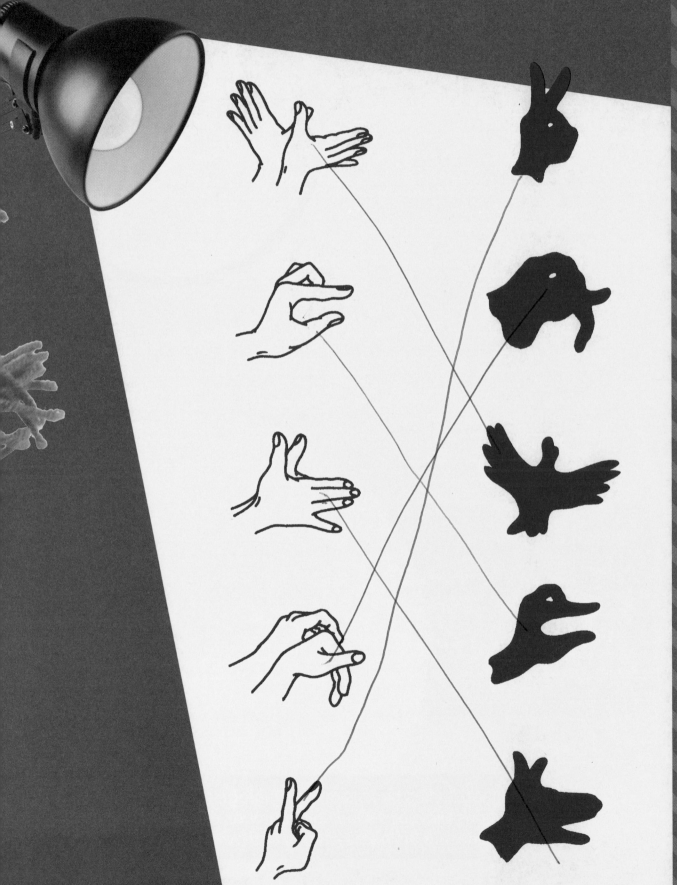

OWLS

by Linda Vasquez

There are about 200 kinds of owls. Some are big. They can be almost three feet long. Some are small. The smallest is as light as a slice of bread.

Hunting

Owls feed on small mammals, insects, birds, and snakes. Most owls hunt at night. That's because owls can see and hear better at night.

An owl may wait on a perch until it hears or sees a small animal. When an owl flies, it is silent. A small animal cannot hear the owl as it swoops down.

Owls hunt at night. Underline the sentence that tells why.

You invite an owl to dinner. Draw three things for it to eat.

A scientist that studies birds is an **ornithologist**. *Ornitho–* means *like a bird*. *Ornithomimus* was an ostrich-like dinosaur. Its name means *bird mimic*.

Seeing and Hearing

Owls have very big eyes. This helps them see in the dark. An owl cannot move its eyes. Instead, it moves its head. It can move its head to look backward, even while it is flying.

If you look at an owl's face, you will see a circle of feathers around its eyes. This circle of feathers is called the facial disc. These feathers send sounds to the owl's ears.

The facial disc helps the owl
_____ better.

Circle the facial disc on the owl.

Nesting

Owls do not build their nests. They may live in an old nest that another bird made. They may live in holes in trees, in ditches, or on ledges of buildings.

Baby owls are called owlets. The eggs do not hatch at the same time, so the owlets in a family may be different sizes. Owlets get very hungry. If there are owlets near you, you might hear them squeak all night as they ask for food.

Five owlets live in this nest.

Owlets in a family may be

_____.

Hungry owlets

_____!

Complete the captions. Then draw pictures.

There is no special name for a baby sea star. But *starlet* sounds nice.

Some owls are endangered. Want to help?

Make owl trading cards. Tell people why owls are awesome.

(Back of card)   (Front of card)

FUN OWL FACTS!

Owls nest _____

_____

Owls hunt _____

_____

Owls hear _____

_____

FUN OWL FACTS!

Owls nest _____

_____

Owls hunt _____

_____

Owls hear _____

_____

April! April!
Are You Here?

by Dora Read Goodale

April! April! are you here?
　　Oh, how fresh the wind is blowing!
See! the sky is bright and clear,
　　Oh, how green the grass is growing!
April! April! are you here?

April! April! is it you?
　　See how fair the flowers are springing!
Sun is warm and brooks are clear,
　　Oh, how glad the birds are singing!
April! April! is it you?

April! April! you are here!
　　Though your smiling turn to weeping,
Though your skies grow cold and drear,
　　Though your gentle winds are sleeping,
April! April! you are here!

What color is used to describe April?

_____

How does April feel? Circle a word.

Weeping means *crying*.

In the poem, it describes the weather. It means:

_____

April! April! is repeated many times. This shows that the speaker is (sad/excited).

I like *July! July!* when the sand is soft and warm beneath my tube feet.

Writing

Snack ATTACK!

Write three words that rhyme with **pear**.

_____

_____

_____

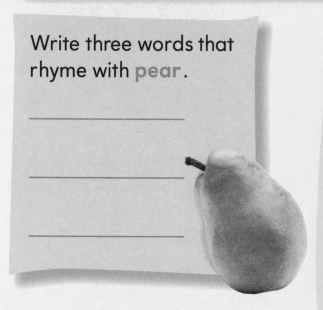

Write three words that rhyme with **toast**.

_____

_____

_____

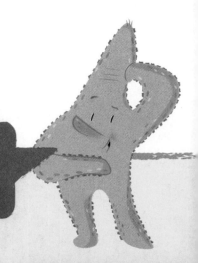

Finish this poem with a rhyming word. Then draw it!

The Snack Attack

by _____

My mother ate an apple

My father ate a pear

My brother ate a sandwich

In his _____!

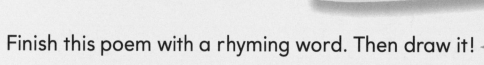

A **rhyme** is when two words end with the same sound. To find a rhyme for *star*, swap out the beginning. Star rhymes with *are*, *car*, and *sandbar*.

I See a POEM

Poets can be inspired by what they see. Look at this artwork. Then describe it.

I see the colors: _____ _____ _____

They make me feel: _____ _____ _____

Now write a poem. You can use some or none of your words.

_____

_____

_____

_____

Bright colors can make you feel *happy* or *excited*. Dark colors can make you feel *calm, sad,* or *scared.*

Being THERE

Rick went camping. Which word makes it easier to imagine what it sounded, smelled, or felt like to be there? **Circle it.**

The forest was	quiet	hushed
The marshmallow was	cooked	toasted
The ground was	rocky	hard
Rick's socks were	wet	damp

Which word tells you about a smell? _____

Both are white. Which one is bright? **Star it.**

Both are big. Which one is towering? **Underline it.**

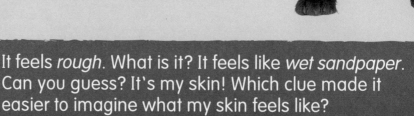

It feels *rough*. What is it? It feels like *wet sandpaper*. Can you guess? It's my skin! Which clue made it easier to imagine what my skin feels like?

"Roger That"

" _____," said _____.

" _____," said _____.

" _____," said _____.

" _____," said _____.

A **dialogue** is when two or more people talk to each other. Their words appear inside quotation marks.

Writing

111

A Good Beginning

A good story grabs a reader's attention in the first few sentences. Circle a good beginning.

Option 1:

Lee and Chloe heard a noise and went inside the house.

Option 2:

Lee and Chloe were playing in their backyard. Then they heard a loud noise, like a roaring monster. They stopped what they were doing and ran into the house.

Option 3:

Lee and Chloe were playing in their backyard when they heard what could only be the roar of the Mangy Monster. They dropped their toys and scurried into the house.

Underline two interesting details in the option you circled.

budge   searching   responded   tiny   whispered
dashed   crept

Escape from the Mangy Monster

Lee and Chloe were playing in their backyard when they heard what could only be the roar of the Mangy Monster. They dropped their toys and scurried into their house. They knew they could hide from the monster in their basement.

But when Lee tried to open the basement door, it wouldn't ~~open~~ _____. "It's locked!" he ~~said~~ _____. So they ~~went~~ _____ into the living room, ~~looking~~ _____ for a place to hide. "What about under the couch?" Chloe asked.

"The Mangy Monster might still get a whiff of our scent if we hide there," Lee ~~said~~ _____. "I know! Let's hide in the attic." So they quietly ~~went~~ _____ upstairs, so as not to make any noise to attract the monster.

The attic door was open! Lee and Chloe both breathed a sigh of relief. From a ~~small~~ _____ window, they saw the Mangy Monster hop past their house. They waited a bit, and then they knew they were safe and went back outside to play.

A Mangy Tale

A story has three parts—a **beginning**, **middle**, and **end**.

solve

characters

problem

solved

setting

The **beginning** introduces the _____, _____, and the _____.

The **middle** tells how the characters work to _____ the problem.

The **end** tells how the problem is _____.

What problem did Lee and Chloe face?

_____

What did they do first to solve their problem?

_____

What did they do next to solve their problem?

_____

How did they finally solve their problem?

_____

A **fictional narrative** is a made-up story. A **personal narrative** is a true story about something that happened to the writer.

Go With the FLOW

Read each paragraph.
Circle the paragraph that flows smoothly.
Box the paragraph that sounds choppy.

My brother got a new dog. He named the dog Missy. My brother feeds the dog. He walks the dog. He plays with the dog. He loves the dog!

My brother got a new dog, and he named it Missy. Every day, my brother feeds, walks, and plays with Missy. He really loves that dog!

Write true or false.

Smooth writing uses a variety of sentence beginnings. _____

Smooth writing uses a variety of sentence types. _____

Smooth writing uses linking words. _____

Smooth writing combines short, choppy sentences

into longer ones. _____

Smooth writing uses a variety of sentence lengths. _____

Don't overthink it! All the statements are true.

What's the STORY?

This picture tells part of a story.

Name the main characters. _____

What problem do they face?

_____

_____

What is the first thing they do to solve the problem?

_____

_____

What is the second thing they do to solve the problem?

_____

_____

How do they finally solve the problem?

_____

_____

What a relief!

Now write the story with dialogue and descriptive words.

Title: _____

_____

_____

_____

_____

_____

_____

_____

_____

Draw a picture to go with the ending of your story.

TELL Your Story

Draw a picture of something that happened to you.

Maybe you ...

... learned how to play the ukulele.

... flew on an airplane for the first time.

... sang or danced in front of people.

... invented a new kind of sandwich.

... saved a bug.

I _____ .

Who were the main people involved? (Don't forget to include yourself.)

_____

_____

What happened first?

_____

_____

What happened next?

_____

_____

What happened last?

_____

_____

How did it make you feel?

_____

_____

What did you learn from it?

_____

_____

Writing

DRAW Your Story

Now tell your story as a comic book. Write dialogue in speech bubbles.

Use a speech bubble—like this one—to show what people are saying out loud!

Wash THAT Dog!

Number the pictures to order the steps for washing a dog.

____

- Fill tub with warm water.
- Gently put dog in tub.
- Shampoo and rinse dog.

____

____

List the supplies needed to wash a dog.

_____

_____

_____

Now tell new dog owners *how* to wash their dogs.

How to _____

Sooner or later, your dog will get stinky! When that happens, it's time to wash the dog.

To wash your dog, you will need _____, _____, and _____. After you gather these supplies, the first step is to _____.

Then, _____. Make sure all of the dog's fur is wet.

Next, _____.

Gently dry the dog with a soft towel. When you are done, your dog will smell like flowers!

Dog before

Dog after

The Gold CARD

You are eligible to apply for a gold library card. You can use it to borrow 100 books at a time. *You are going to need a bigger backpack.*

Gold Library Card Membership

My name is:

I recommend this book:

Here is a summary of what happens in the book.

Here are two reasons why I like the book.

☐ I really mean it. You should read this book.

RSVP

Did you ever see *RSVP* at the bottom of an invitation? It means *please respond*. (Are you coming to the party or not?)

Sometimes, your teacher asks you to respond to a story. Read the responses below. Can you guess what the original question was?

How _____

_____ at the end

of the story?

R.S.V.P.
At the end of the story, I think the townspeople started to feel respect for Jack. In the beginning, they laughed at him when he traded a cow for beans. They were not laughing at him now.

R.S.V.P.
At the end of the story, the townspeople felt surprised. A giant chased Jack down the beanstalk. Jack was telling the truth all along!

The first sentence in a good response always restates the prompt. Look for similar words in both RSVPs.

Break a Sweat

You want everyone to exercise. Circle the statement that tells your opinion and gives a good reason for it.

People should exercise.

Exercise is hard work and takes a lot of time, but it is fun.

If you want to feel great and have fun, I know how: Exercise!

A lot of people do not like to exercise, but they should do it anyway.

Persuasive writing convinces the reader to agree with your opinion. Always give a **good reason** for your opinion and be **positive**.

Color in the reasons that will convince people to agree with you.

1 ⬭ Exercise makes your muscles and bones healthy.

2 ⬭ Exercise keeps your mind active.

3 ⬭ Exercise can make you feel sore the next day.

4 ⬭ Exercising is a fun way to spend time with your friends.

5 ⬭ Exercise can hurt you if you overdo it.

Read each example. Which reason above does it support? Write the number.

_____ Playing soccer, dancing, and jumping rope are more fun with friends.

_____ Having an active mind might help you pay more attention in school. Or even get better grades!

_____ Your heart is a muscle, so exercising can keep it healthy too!

Keep SUMMER?

Should school go year round?
Or should kids have the summer off?

Check the reasons you agree with each opinion.

Year round

- ☐ Kids won't forget what they learned over the summer.

- ☐ Kids will learn more if they go to school all year.

- ☐ Kids can see their friends more often if they go to school all year.

Summers off

- ☐ Kids need time to play and rest.

- ☐ Kids won't have as much time with their extended family, like cousins and grandparents, if they go to school all year.

- ☐ Kids won't be able to do other things, like go to camp or go on vacation, if they go to school all year.

Now share your opinion. **Write a persuasive letter to the principal.**

Dear Principal _____,

I think that _____

_____

_____

_____

_____

_____

_____

Sincerely,

_____

I was persuasive!

☐ I stated my **opinion.**

☐ I wrote **reasons** to support my opinion.

☐ I restated my **opinion.**

☐ I asked the reader to **agree** or **take some action.**

Picture YOUR OPINION!

Attach a chart or graph to your letter. **Circle the one that supports your opinion.**

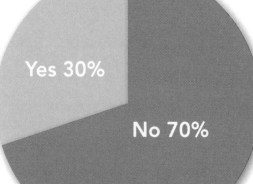

Want Year-Round School (Kids)

Yes 30%

No 70%

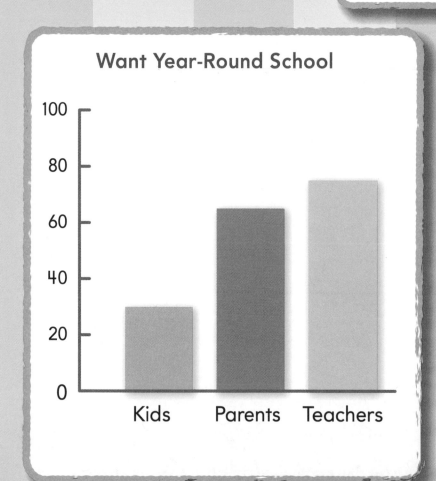

Want Year-Round School

Kids   Parents   Teachers

Finding FACTS

The *Amphibian Journal* asks you to write a report about salamanders.

Circle useful facts and details from *The Animal Book.*

Salamanders are amphibians, like frogs.

Baby salamanders have gills.

Many North American salamanders do not have lungs.

Snakes eat rats.

Over 900 different kinds of birds live in the United States.

About 100 different kinds of salamanders live in the United States.

The largest salamander can grow up to two feet long.

The blue whale is the largest mammal.

Salamanders live in moist, dark places, like under logs.

There are many interesting facts in the world. You can find them on the Internet, in books, in videos, and (most likely) in your head!

Slippery Facts

Salamanders can be secretive. But their facts aren't!
Write some salamander facts on these notecards.

Salamanders—life cycle

Fact: _____

_____

_____

Source: Krim, Mary. The Animal Book. New York: Lonhouse Books. 2012. p. 42

Salamanders—habitat

Fact: _____

_____

_____

Source: Krim, Mary. The Animal Book. New York: Lonhouse Books. 2012. p. 42

Salamanders—other facts

Fact: _____

_____

_____

Source: Krim, Mary. The Animal Book. New York: Lonhouse Books. 2012. p. 42

If you write down the exact words from a source, put quotation marks around them. Always include a **source** for every fact you note.

Mistake Proof!

Your report is almost done. It's time to find and fix mistakes.
Circle punctuation, capitalization, spelling, and grammar mistakes.

Salamanders!

Salamanders are verry interesting animals. They comes in all different sizes and colors and can be found just about anywhere.

Salamanders have a fascinating lifecycle. Like frogs, salamanders are amphibians? Some salamanders lay their eggs in lakes or ponds. When the eggs hatch, the little salamanders have gills to help them breath under water. As salamanders grow, they lose their gills and breathe aire. Then they leave the pond and walk on land.

About 100 different kinds of salamanders lives in the United States. The Great smoky Mountains National Park is known as the "Salamander Capital of the World." This is because so many different kinds of salamanders live in the park.

The largest salamander in the united States is called the hellbender. It can grow up to two feet long! These salamanders are very hard to find because they only come out at night . . .

Salamanders are very cool animals. Would you like to sees one? next time you are out hiking, turn over some rotten logs. You just might find a salamander hiding there!

Psst. A little seabird told me that there are two mistakes in each paragraph.

POWER Report

The *Amphibian Journal* wants you to present your report to a group of scientists. **Make two slides.**

SLIDE 1

Write a title. Draw a picture to show the main idea.

SLIDE 2

Write an interesting fact. Draw a picture to illustrate the fact.

Threatened and Endangered Amphibian Species in the United States

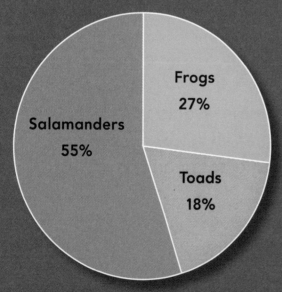

Salamanders 55%
Frogs 27%
Toads 18%

You add this final slide to your presentation. What will you say about it? **Check one.**

☐ There are more salamanders than frogs and toads combined.

☐ Salamanders are the most endangered species in the U.S.

☐ Salamanders are the most endangered amphibian species in the U.S.

STRETCH
Before You Write

Before you write, ask yourself three questions.
(You can whisper them if you like.)

Who am I writing for?

Why am I writing?

What am I writing?

Now read the prompts below.

Circle **who** you are writing for.

Put a box around **why** you are writing.

Make a ☆ above **what** you are writing.

Your lunchroom makes a lot of waste. Every day, kids throw away plastic bottles, cans, and cartons. Write a letter to your principal to persuade him or her to start a recycling program in the lunchroom.

You have a new baby brother. Write a short informational paragraph to tell him how to be a *great* baby brother. Explain how you like your socks folded, your bed made, and your tarantula tank cleaned.

Freewrite it, BABY!

Freewriting is when you write without rules. Just write whatever comes to mind. *Don't worry about grammar and punctuation.*

Teddy freewrote this. After, he circled the important ideas.

I want to (persuade) the (principal) to let third-graders have (recess) again. I don't like sitting for such a long time. I get (stiff) and (sleepy.) Other students get (grumpy.) The principal is far away from my room. Maybe I can send a (note?)

Now it's your turn. Start freewriting a **song**, a **story**, or a **letter**. Then go back and circle important ideas.

_____

_____

_____

_____

_____

_____

Multiplication
and
Division

Leo's Lunch

Leo can **add** or **multiply** to get an equal number of ingredients.

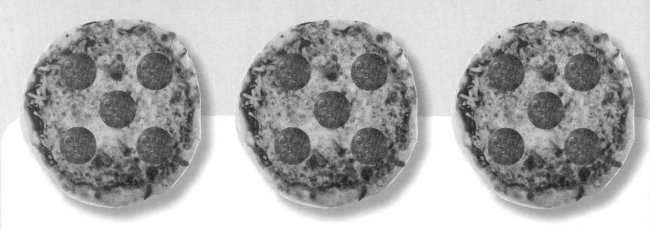

Leo makes **3** pizzas. Each has **5** pepperoni slices.

How many pepperoni slices are there in all?

Add: ___5___ + ___5___ + ___5___ = _____

Multiply: ___3___ × ___5___ = _____

Now draw 2 x 5. That's **2** pizzas with **5** pepperonis each.

Multiplying is adding the same number, again and again.

C🍪unter

There are **5** glasses. Leo adds **4** ice cubes to each glass.

How many ice cubes are there in all?

Add: _____ + _____ + _____ + _____ + _____ = _____

Multiply: _____ × _____ = _____

Leo serves **6** ice cream cones. He adds **2** scoops to each cone.

How many scoops are there in all?

Add: ____ + ____ + ____ + ____ + ____ + ____ = ____

Multiply: _____ × _____ = _____

HUGE SALE!
Tiny Toys!

The sale starts today!

Sal is selling **24** toy soldiers. She has **4** bins. Draw an equal number of soldiers in each bin. Make an **X** for each soldier.

There are _____ soldiers in all.

There are _____ soldiers in each bin.

There are _____ equal groups.

Hint: Make an X in each bin until there are 24.

Dan is selling **15** planes. He has **3** bins. Draw an equal number of planes in each bin. Make an **X** for each plane.

How many planes are in each bin? $15 \div 3 =$ _____

My cousin Gareth split his bag of oyster chips with me equally. He gave me 11 chips. How many chips were in the bag?

Carol is selling **32** duckies. She has **4** buckets.
Draw an equal number of duckies in each bin.
Make an **X** for each duckie.

There are _____ duckies in all.

There are _____ duckies in each bucket.

There are _____ equal groups.

$32 \div 4 =$ _____

Dana is selling fish. If the equation is **9 ÷ 3 = 3**, then:

There are _____ fish in all.

There are _____ fish in each bucket.

There are _____ equal groups.

Draw it! Make an **X** for each fish.

Gold Mine!

It's Gold Rush Day at Camp Midas!
Campers pan for gold in the streams.

Tara uses **2** pans to sift for gold.
She finds **8** nuggets in each pan.

Draw them.

_____ pans of _____ nuggets is **16** nuggets.

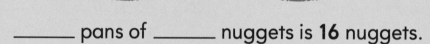

_____ × _____ = **16** nuggets

Carter uses **4** pans. He finds **4** gold nuggets in each pan.

Draw them.

_____ × _____ = _____ nuggets

Ingrid uses **2** pans. She finds **3** gold nuggets in each.

_____ x _____ = _____ nuggets

Draw Ingrid's pans with nuggets.

Thomas is rich! He uses **4** pans. He finds **9** gold nuggets in each.

_____ x _____ = _____ nuggets

Draw Thomas's pans with nuggets.

Who found more nuggets? Martin or Reno?

Martin found **9** nuggets in each of his **2** pans.

_____ x _____ = _____ nuggets

Reno found **7** nuggets in each of his **4** pans.

_____ x _____ = _____ nuggets

Pay Day!

The campers turn in their gold nuggets for rolls of coins.

Andrew gets **4** rolls of **5** coins.

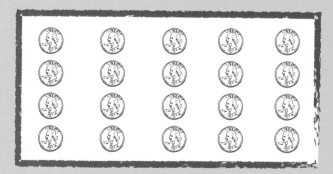

He has _____ coins in all.

_____ × _____ = _____ coins

Marie gets **2** rolls of **5** coins. **Draw them.**

She has _____ coins in all.

_____ × _____ = _____ coins

An **array** is when you arrange things in rows and columns. A row goes across. A column goes down.

Raul has been going to Camp Midas for four summers. The first summer, he takes home:

_____5_____ × _____8_____ = _____ coins

Draw it as an array. (Hint: That's 5 rows of 8 coins.)

The second summer, Raul takes home:

_____7_____ × _____5_____ = _____ coins

Draw it as an array. (Hint: That's 7 rows of 5 coins.)

The third summer, Raul takes home:

_____5_____ × _____6_____ = _____ coins

Draw it as an array.

Hut, Hut, Hana!

Hana catches the ball at the **0**-yard line.

She runs past **3** lines. There are **5** yards between each line. How far did she run?

Start at **0**. Trace **3** jumps.

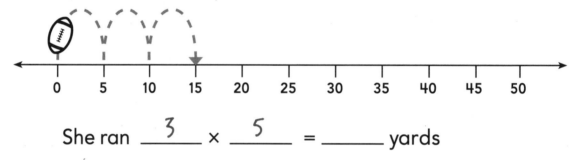

She ran ___3___ × ___5___ = _____ yards

Otto catches the ball at the **25**-yard line. He runs toward the goal.

He runs past **3** lines. How far did he run?

Start at **25**. Draw **3** jumps.

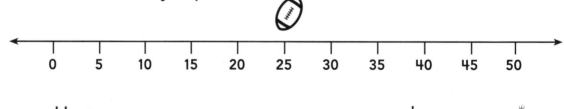

He ran _____ × _____ = _____ yards

Hana and Otto ran the same distance.
They just started at different places.

MUMMY ESCAPE!

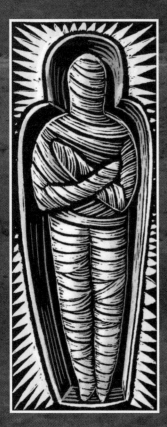

The mummies escaped from the pyramids!

Quick! Solve these problems to climb to the top of the pyramid! It's safe there (and the view is spectacular).

The missing number is the product of the two numbers below it.

Bailey cat sits for **5** days. He brushes Bo **2** times a day.

In all, he brushes Bo ___5___ x ___2___ times.

Trace **5** jumps of **2**.

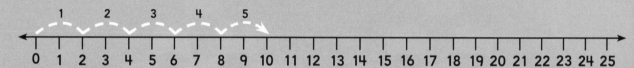

The number you land on is the total number of times Bailey brushed Bo.

Bailey brushes Bo _____ times.

Bailey cat sits for **5** days.

He feeds Bo **3** meals a day.

In all, he feeds Bo _____ x _____ times.

Draw _____ jumps of _____.

Bailey feeds Bo _____ times.

Whiskers

Bo is **polydactyl** (pah-lee-dac-til). He has **6** toes on each foot.

In all, Bo has _____ × __6__ toes.

Draw _____ jumps of _____.

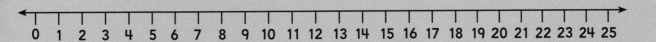

Bo has _____ toes.

Use the number line to complete this interesting fact about Bo.

Bo entered _____ cat shows. He won _____ ribbons in each!

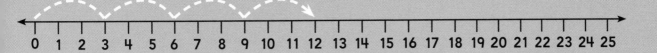

Math

Draw each problem. Then solve it.
Match the answer to a secret letter.

7 x 5	8 x 3	4 x 6	2 x 8
Draw an array.	Draw an array.	Draw equal groups.	Draw equal groups.

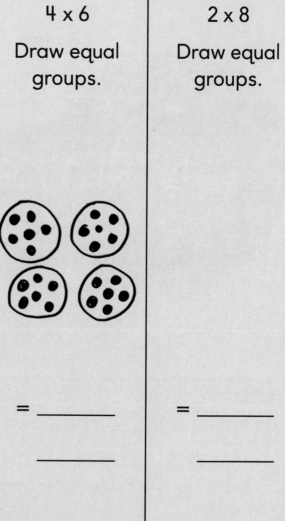

= 35

G

= ___

___

= ___

___

= ___

___

Motto!

Draw a line from the number line to the matching problem.

Solve each problem. Then match the answer to a letter.

$$\begin{array}{r} 4 \\ \times 9 \\ \hline \end{array} \qquad \begin{array}{r} 6 \\ \times 7 \\ \hline \end{array} \qquad \begin{array}{r} 8 \\ \times 2 \\ \hline \end{array} \qquad \begin{array}{r} 10 \\ \times 5 \\ \hline \end{array} \qquad \begin{array}{r} 7 \\ \times 3 \\ \hline \end{array}$$

___ ___ ___ ___ ___ !

The code is: 32/D, 50/E, 35/G, 42/I, 16/M, 24/O, 21/S, 36/T.

Run, Cookie, Run!

Shay bakes **18** gingerbread men. Each time he opens the oven door, **6** run away.

Now the oven is empty!
How many times did Shay open it?

6 run away at a time. **Circle groups of 6.**

Count the groups. Shay opened the oven _____ times.

Now **subtract** to find the answer!

There are 18. 6 run away! **Cross out 6.**

Write how many are left.

18
−6
☐

Now there are 12. 6 run away! **Cross out 6.**

Write how many are left.

12
−6
☐

Now there are 6. 6 run away! **Cross them out.**

6
−6
☐

Write how many are left.

I subtracted _____ times until **0** were left. So, 18 ÷ 6 = _____.

Shay bakes **8** gingerbread babies. **4** crawl out of the oven each time he opens it.

Now the oven is empty! How many times did Shay open it?

Make an **X** for each baby. **Draw a line through 4.**

Subtract

Write how many are left.

Make an **X** for each baby left. **Draw a line through 4.**

Write how many are left.

I subtracted _____ times until **0** were left. So, 8 ÷ 4 = _____.

Smile! It's class picture day.

Ms. Wimple's class has **20** kids.
They line up in **4** rows of **5** kids.

Mr. Davis's class has **20** kids, too.
They line up in **5** rows of **4** kids.

_____ equal groups of **5**

$\boxed{5}$ + $\boxed{}$ + $\boxed{}$ + $\boxed{}$ = 20

_____ equal groups of **4**

$\boxed{4}$ + $\boxed{}$ + $\boxed{}$ + $\boxed{}$ + $\boxed{}$ = 20

$$4 \times 5 = 20 \quad \textbf{is the same as} \quad 5 \times 4 = 20$$

Write a multiplication sentence to describe each picture.
Then write it in a different way!

  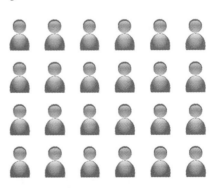

_____ × _____ = _____   _____ × _____ = _____   _____ × _____ = _____

_____ × _____ = _____   _____ × _____ = _____   _____ × _____ = _____

Ray's Roundup

Ray uses a lasso to round up his toys.

There is a **12** cow stampede. **Draw loops around groups of 2.**

There are _____ groups of 2. So, _12_ ÷ _2_ = _____

Do you want to share 10 snails with me? First I'll draw
10. Then I'll circle groups of 2. I made 5 groups!
10 ÷ 2 = 5. Eat up, my friend!

There is a **24** elephant stampede. **Draw loops around groups of 4.**

There are _____ groups of 4. So, _24_ ÷ _4_ = _____

There is a **14** goat stampede. **Draw loops around groups of 7.**

There are _____ groups of 7. So, _____ ÷ _____ = _____

Skipping

Zach and Carly skipped stones.

Zach's first throw landed 24 feet into the pond.
Each skip was 4 feet long.

How many skips did it make?

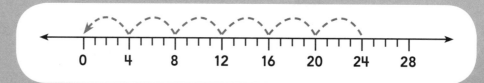

Count the number of skips the stone made from 24 down to 0.

It made _____ skips.

So, ___24___ ÷ ___4___ = _____ skips.

Carly's first throw landed 32 feet into the
pond. Each skip was 8 feet long.

How many skips did it make?

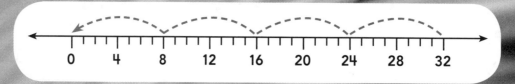

It made _____ skips from 32 down to 0.

So, _____ ÷ _____ = _____ skips.

Stones

Zach's second throw landed 40 feet into the pond. Each skip was 5 feet long.

How many skips did it make?

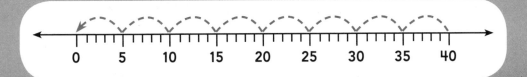

It made _____ skips from 40 down to 0.

So, _____ ÷ _____ = _____ skips.

Carly's second throw landed 28 feet into the pond. Each skip was 4 feet long.

How many skips did it make?

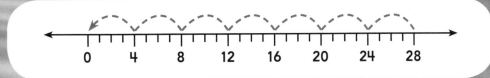

It made _____ skips from 28 down to 0.

So, _____ ÷ _____ = _____ skips.

A skipping stone bounces off the water. Here's how you do it. Find a flat stone. Throw it low and fast. Give it some spin! *Bounce, bounce, bounce.* You're a natural.

Math Craft!

Rosie has **24** squares of fabric. She wants to make a quilt with **6** squares in each row.

How many rows of 6 can she make? **Draw a picture.**

She can make _____ rows of 6 squares.

A row goes across. At the underwater Sea-plex, there are 10 seats in a row. (I usually sit next to Gareth.)

Arden has **18** squares of fabric. He wants to make a quilt with **6** squares in each row.

How many rows of 6 can he make?

Draw a picture.

He can make _____ rows of 6 squares.

Arden lends you **20** squares of fabric.
Make a quilt with **4** rows.

How many squares are in each row?

Draw a picture.

There are _____ squares in each row.

So, there are 4 rows of _____ in 20.

Everyone loves your quilt.
Write the pattern as a division equation.

_____ ÷ _____ = _____

The Unknown Factor!

Lily collected **20** snow globes from places she visited. She has **5** shelves.

She wants to display the same number of globes on each shelf.

She writes it as a problem. $5 \times g = 20$

g is the unknown factor! Find out what *g* is.

Draw one globe on each shelf until there are 20 globes.

Count the number of snow globes on each shelf. That is *g*.

$$5 \times \underline{\hspace{2cm}} = 20$$

So, Lily puts _____ globes on each shelf.

g is a placeholder for the number of globes on each shelf.

Lily's brother has **24** autographed baseballs. He has **3** shelves.

He wants to display the same number of baseballs on each shelf.

   She writes it as a problem. $3 \times b = 24$

Find out what **b** is!

Draw one ball on each shelf until there are 24 balls.

_____

_____

_____

Count the number of baseballs on each shelf. That is b.

   $3 \times \underline{\hspace{1cm}} = 24$

   So, Lily puts _____ baseballs on each shelf.

Now find these unknown factors:

$36 = 4 \times z$ $s \times 8 = 56$ $r \times 5 = 45$ $12 = 3 \times p$

$z = \underline{\hspace{1cm}}$ $s = \underline{\hspace{1cm}}$ $r = \underline{\hspace{1cm}}$ $p = \underline{\hspace{1cm}}$

I have a collection, too! Can you autograph this baseball for me?

Ms. Wimple's class makes a vegetable garden behind the school.

Ms. Wimple's Garden

Write the number of vegetables in each plot.

2 × 8 plot = _____ carrots

6 × 4 plot = _____ beets

5 × 5 plot = _____ tomatoes

3 × 7 plot = _____ squash

3 × 4 plot = _____ radishes

3 × 8 plot = _____ cabbages

Now label the plots.

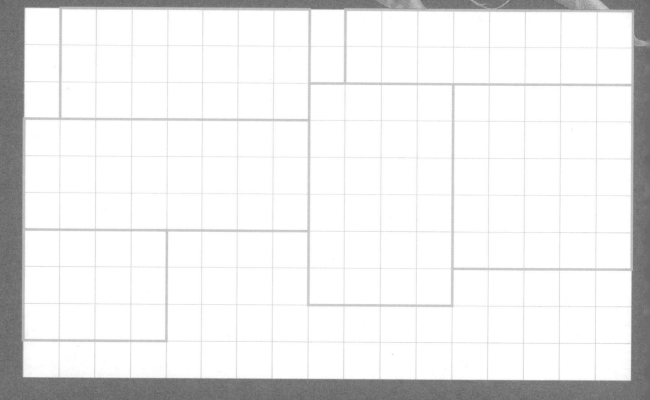

Add a 5 x 3 plot for bush beans. Then label it!

Clyde, the cookie cutter, is a cutup.
He loves to tell jokes!

Solve each problem to finish Clyde's joke.

1. $(5 \times 2) + (1 \times 3) =$ ☐

2. $(5 \times 3) + (7 \times 2) =$ ☐

3. $(7 \times 3) - (2 \times 5) =$ ☐

4. $(3 \times 6) - (4 \times 2) =$ ☐

5. $(2 \times 3) + (4 \times 2) =$ ☐

6. $(5 \times 4) + (3 \times 3) =$ ☐

7. $(9 \times 3) - (9 \times 2) =$ ☐

8. $(1 \times 3) + (3 \times 6) =$ ☐

9. $(3 \times 5) + (8 \times 2) =$ ☐

10. $(3 \times 9) - (6 \times 2) =$ ☐

11. $(3 \times 3) + (3 \times 2) =$ ☐

12. $(4 \times 2) + (9 \times 3) =$ ☐

Why did the cookie go to the doctor?

__ __ __ __ __ __ __ __ __ __ __ __ !

1	2	3	4	5	6	7	8	9	10	11	12

A	B	C	E	F	I	L	M	N	O	R	S	T	U	W	Y
7	8	9	10	11	13	14	15	16	20	21	28	29	31	33	35

Multiply the numbers inside the
parentheses first. Then add or subtract.

Mr. Zero and Mr. One

Do you want to hang out with Mr. Zero and Mr. One?
Of course you do.

Show them you can multiply and divide by their rules.

The product of 0 and any number is _____.

So, 4 × 0 = _____.

The product of any number and 1 is _____.

So, 4 × 1 = _____.

Any number divided by 1 equals _____.

So, 5 ÷ 1 = _____.

Any number divided by itself equals _____.

So, 5 ÷ 5 = _____.

0 divided by any number except 0 equals _____.

So, 0 ÷ 5 = _____ .

You cannot divide by _____.

10 × 1 = _____   0 ÷ 4 = _____   1 × 0 = _____

24 ÷ 1 = _____   45 ÷ 45 = _____

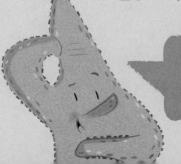

Mr. Zero and Mr. One are fun. But Mr.
Five is better. It's the size of my sweater.

Lightning Pong!

Lightning Pong is fast. To keep score, you need to multiply and divide fast.

21 spins!

There are **7** balls in each row.

3 rows of 7 = 21

So, 21 ÷ 3 = 7

It's your serve.

Complete these multiplication and division sentences.

24 loops!

27 smashes!

64 time outs!

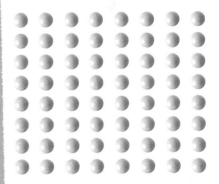

6 rows of _____ = 24

_____ x _____ = 24

24 ÷ _____ = _____

3 rows of _____ = 27

3 x _____ = 27

27 ÷ 3 = _____

8 rows of _____ = 64

8 x _____ = 64

64 ÷ 8 = _____

On a Roll!

Your donut rolled away! Get it back. Draw a line through numbers that can be divided by 2 with none left over. (You can move in any direction, including diagonally.)

Start at 2 and end at 24. Get rolling!

2	67	40	13	17	67	9
13	10	71	22	33	91	19
49	11	49	17	66	81	93
101	23	39	311	47	16	113
53	1	51	3	46	31	21
24	42	12	38	7	1	19

How many numbers from 1 through 100 can be divided by 2 with none left over?

Are those numbers **even** or **odd**?

If you find your donut in less than 5 minutes, you can still eat it. That's the five-minute rule.

A Murder of Crows

There are **3 flocks** of crows.
Each flock has **9 crows**.
How many crows are there in all?

First draw 3 flocks of 9.

Skip-count by **9s** to find the total.   _____ , _____ , _____

So, 3 × 9 = _____ crows

Shh! A roost is a group of sleeping crows. There are **5 roosts** of crows. Each roost has **6 crows**. How many crows are there in all?

First draw 5 roosts of 6.

Skip-count by **6s** to find the total.

_____ , _____ , _____ , _____ , _____

So, 5 × 6 = _____ crows

Poets call a flock of crows a **murder**. A crow is one of the smartest animals on earth. Next time you see one, ask it for homework help, as they are also known to be caring.

An Apple a Day!

Each day, the dragon snacked on apples from the orchard. How many days did it take to finish them all?

The Gala tree had 36 apples. The dragon ate 9 apples a day. Subtract 9 as many times as you can until there are 0 left.

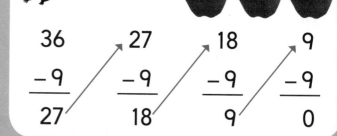

$$\begin{array}{r} 36 \\ -9 \\ \hline 27 \end{array} \qquad \begin{array}{r} 27 \\ -9 \\ \hline 18 \end{array} \qquad \begin{array}{r} 18 \\ -9 \\ \hline 9 \end{array} \qquad \begin{array}{r} 9 \\ -9 \\ \hline 0 \end{array}$$

9 was subtracted 4 times. The apples were gone in _____ days.

The Honeycrunch tree had 18 apples. The dragon ate 9 apples a day. Subtract 9 as many times as you can until there are 0 left.

The apples were gone in _____ days. So, 18 ÷ 9 = _____.

The Snow Apple tree had 36 apples. The dragon ate 6 apples a day. Subtract 6 as many times as you can until there are 0 left.

The apples were gone in _____ days. So, 36 ÷ 6 = _____.

The dragon ate 48 apples in 8 days. Subtract to solve
48 ÷ 8.

She ate _____ apples a day.

The dragon ate 45 apples in 9 days. Subtract to solve
45 ÷ 9.

She ate _____ apples a day.

Lockout!

Oh, snap! Someone mixed up the locks on the school lockers.

Use the multiplication table to find each combination. **Here's how.**

Think of each division problem as a multiplication problem.

$30 \div 10 = \boxed{}$ **is the same as** $10 \times \boxed{} = 30$

10 is the first factor. Find it in the table. **30** is the product. Find it. Look up, to the top row. The unknown factor is **3**.

×	0	1	2	3	4	5	6	7	8	9	10
0	0	0	0	0	0	0	0	0	0	0	0
1	0	1	2	3	4	5	6	7	8	9	10
2	0	2	4	6	8	10	12	14	16	18	20
3	0	3	6	9	12	15	18	21	24	27	30
4	0	4	8	12	16	20	24	28	32	36	40
5	0	5	10	15	20	25	30	35	40	45	50
6	0	6	12	18	24	30	36	42	48	54	60
7	0	7	14	21	28	35	42	49	56	63	70
8	0	8	16	24	32	40	48	56	64	72	80
9	0	9	18	27	36	45	54	63	72	81	90
10	0	10	20	30	40	50	60	70	80	90	100

Find each combination.

$25 \div 5$	$64 \div 8$	$21 \div 3$	$36 \div 6$	$42 \div 6$	$7 \div 7$
____	____	____	____	____	____

$40 \div 8$	$54 \div 6$	$30 \div 3$	$63 \div 7$	$21 \div 3$	$72 \div 9$
____	____	____	____	____	____

Musical Hats!

The Musical Hats are marching in the parade. Each musician wears a hat.

How many hats will they need to perform?

There are **2** rows of flute players. Each row has **7** players. How many flute players are there in all?

_____ × _____ = _____ flute players

There are **6** rows of drummers. Each row has **4** drummers. How many drummers are there in all?

_____ × _____ = _____ drummers

There are **3** rows of trumpet players with **5** in each row. How many trumpet players are there in all?

_____ × _____ = _____ trumpet players

The Musical Hats need:

_____ + _____ + _____ = _____ hats in all!

L♡ve Punch!

Sherbet Punch (1 pitcher)
Mix:
- 1 can of pineapple juice
- 1 bottle of ginger ale
- 6 scoops of sherbet

Tova wants to make punch for her class Valentine's Day party.

The recipe is for **1** pitcher. She needs to make **6** for the class.

Multiply to complete the table.

Number of Pitchers	1	2	3	4	5	6
Cans of pineapple juice	1	2				
Bottles of ginger ale	1	2				
Scoops of sherbet	6	12				

Make a list of ingredients she needs to make **6 pitchers**.

_____ cans of pineapple juice

_____ bottles of ginger ale

_____ scoops of sherbet

How many bottles of ginger ale do you need to make **3 pitchers**? _____ bottles

How many scoops of sherbet do you need to make **5 pitchers**? _____ scoops

Cool Clues!

What do you call a penguin in the desert?
Answer the clues to solve the riddle!

I have 4 factors.
Three of my factors are 1, 2, and 10.
What is my fourth factor?

 = _____

I have 5 factors.
Some of my factors are 4, 8, and 2.
What product am I?

☐ = _____

I have 8 factors.
3, 4, 6, and 8 are four of them!
What product am I?

☐ = _____

I am 35. One of my factors is 5.
What is my next highest factor?

☐ = _____

I told the penguins I would keep their code safe.
24 = S, 5 = L, 16 = O, 7 = T

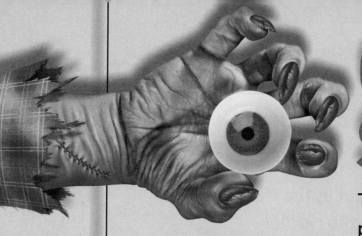

Ghoul School

The kids at Ghoul School are planning a spooktacular bash!

Vigo has **3 new jars of eyeballs**. Each jar has the same number of eyeballs. His sister gives him **4** more eyeballs. Now he has **28**.

How many eyeballs are in each jar?

Solve it in two steps.

First, subtract the **4** eyeballs his sister gave him.

28 − 4 = ⬜ eyeballs

Remember that each jar has the same number. So, divide **24** eyeballs by **3**. Draw one eyeball in each jar until there are 24.

There are ⬜ eyeballs in each jar. So, 24 ÷ 3 = ⬜

If a problem looks tricky, ask yourself: *What do I need to know? What information do I have? How will I solve the problem?* That's how I opened a jar of sea pickles last week.

Rana has **35 monster masks**. **8** of them were gifts. She bought the rest over **3** years.

If Rana bought the same number of masks each year, how many did she buy last year?

First, figure out **how many** masks Rana bought.

☐	–	☐	=	☐
total number of masks		masks that were gifts		masks Rana bought

Then **divide them by 3**, the number of years over which she bought them.

☐	÷	☐	=	☐
masks Rana bought		years that she bought them		how many each year

Hazel has **$25** to spend on cauldrons. Her mom gives her **$5** more. Each cauldron costs **$6**.

How many can she buy? (Work it out below.)

Boris has **24 feet of spider web**. He cuts it into **9** pieces. Each piece is **2** feet long.

How much is left over? (Work it out below.)

Sea Dragon!

Snap the sea dragon buys a boogie board for $4. He also buys 5 beach balls for $2 each.

How much money does he spend?

He spends $4 + 5 \times 2$ dollars.

Circle the next step. (Hint: Follow the order of operations.)

add $4 + 5$ multiply 5×2

Snap buys a bathing cap for $5. He also buys 6 sand shovels for $3 each.

How much money does he spend?

He spends _____ + _____ × _____ dollars.

Circle the correct order of operations.

add, then multiply   multiply, then add

Snap's brother Stevie buys 2 swimsuits for $8 each. Then he buys a pair of $5 swim goggles.

How much money does he spend?

_____ × _____ + _____ = _____

Follow the **order of operations**. First, multiply and divide from left to right. Then, add and subtract from left to right.

Number and Operations in Base 10

FREE RANGE

FRANKIE

Frankie wants to know about how many eggs her chickens laid.

Estimate to find a number close to the exact amount.

73 → __75__ brown eggs

+ 21 → +25 white eggs

about [ ] eggs

Here's one way!
Find **compatible** numbers that are easy to add.

42 → ____   23 → ____   52 → ____

+ 36 → +____   + 99 → +____   + 39 → +____

[ ]   [ ]   [ ]

Now **round up or down** to the nearest hundred.

214 → __200__   214 is closer to 200 than 300.

+ 678 → +700   678 is closer to 700 than 600.

about [ ] eggs

523 → ____   254 → ____   235 → ____

+ 117 → +____   + 167 → +____   + 374 → +____

[ ]   [ ]   [ ]

To round to the nearest hundred, look at the tens digit. In 2<u>1</u>4, 1 is less than 5. So, **round down** to 200. In 6<u>7</u>8, 7 is more than 5. So **round up** to 700.

Frankie sells her eggs at the farmer's market.
About how many does she have left?

Find **compatible** numbers that
are easy to subtract.

$$78 \rightarrow \underline{75} \quad \text{cartons}$$
$$-47 \rightarrow \underline{-50} \quad \text{cartons sold}$$

about [ ] left

$40 \rightarrow \underline{\quad}$	$92 \rightarrow \underline{\quad}$	$68 \rightarrow \underline{\quad}$
$-13 \rightarrow \underline{-\quad}$	$-65 \rightarrow \underline{-\quad}$	$-31 \rightarrow \underline{-\quad}$
[ ]	[ ]	[ ]

Now **round up or down** to subtract.

$$687 \rightarrow \underline{700} \quad \text{687 is closer to 700 than 600.}$$
$$-516 \rightarrow \underline{-500} \quad \text{516 is closer to 500 than 600.}$$

about [ ] left

$517 \rightarrow \underline{\quad}$	$776 \rightarrow \underline{\quad}$	$445 \rightarrow \underline{\quad}$
$-249 \rightarrow \underline{-\quad}$	$-384 \rightarrow \underline{-\quad}$	$-112 \rightarrow \underline{-\quad}$
[ ]	[ ]	[ ]

Frankie has 72 Leghorn chickens and
83 Plymouth Rock chickens. About how
many chickens does she have?

about [ ] chickens

A NEW RECORD!

Rewrite these world records in the **expanded form** and the **word form**.

In 2008, a group of Romanian school kids wrote the longest letter to Santa - **1,357** feet long!

Expand it:
1000 + 300 + 50 + 7

Use words:
one thousand, three hundred fifty-seven

In 2010, a fourth grader in Warwick, NY wore the most underpants at one time - **215** pairs!

Expand it:

_____

Use words:

_____

215 pairs!

1,301!

In 2013, Canadian kids lined up the most carved pumpkins - **1,301**!

Expand it:

_____

Use words:

_____

In **expanded form**, write the number as **thousands** plus **hundreds** plus **tens** plus **ones**. So, 1,469 is 1000 + 400 + 60 + 9.

In 2013, **288** people joined the largest reading lesson in the United Kingdom.

Expand it:

_____

Use words:

_____

288 people!

In 2012, a dog shelter in Hungary gathered the most plush toys - **6,540**!

Expand it:

_____

Use words:

_____

6,540!

What world record do you want to set?

_____

_____

_____

Expand it: _____

Use words: _____

There are more than two thousand kinds of sea stars. Let's say there are two thousand, one hundred fifty-two. That's 2,152.

BETTY'S in BUSINESS

Betty makes bead necklaces.

She has **352** beads.
She uses **167** beads to make a necklace.

Estimate how many beads she has left.

352 – 167 ⟶ _____ – _____

about _____ beads left

Now use place value to find **exactly** how many beads she has left.

First subtract the **ones**.
There are not enough ones to subtract!
So, regroup **5 tens** and **2 ones** as
4 tens and **12 ones**.

$$\begin{array}{r} \overset{4\ 12}{3\cancel{5}\cancel{2}} \\ -\ 167 \\ \hline 5 \end{array}$$

Now subtract the **tens**.
There are not enough tens to subtract!
So, regroup **3 hundreds** and **4 tens** as
2 hundreds and **14 tens**.

$$\begin{array}{r} \overset{14}{\overset{2\ \cancel{4}\ 12}{\cancel{3}\cancel{5}\cancel{2}}} \\ -\ 167 \\ \hline 85 \end{array}$$

Finally, subtract the **hundreds**.

$$\begin{array}{r} \overset{14}{\overset{2\ \cancel{4}\ 12}{\cancel{3}\cancel{5}\cancel{2}}} \\ -\ 167 \\ \hline 185 \end{array}$$

exactly _____ beads left

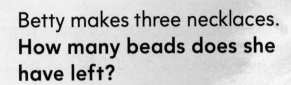

Betty makes three necklaces. **How many beads does she have left?**

Estimate: [ ]
537
− 123
[ ]

Estimate: [ ]
268
− 157
[ ]

Estimate: [ ]
426
− 218
[ ]

A herd of unicorns orders matching rainbow necklaces.

How many beads does she have left?

Estimate: [ ]
354
− 206
[ ]

Estimate: [ ]
679
− 482
[ ]

Estimate: [ ]
787
− 378
[ ]

Estimate: [ ]
615
− 342
[ ]

Estimate: [ ]
607
− 568
[ ]

Estimate: [ ]
973
− 869
[ ]

FAST MATH TRICK!

Christopher and his pet mouse, Leo, perform math magic.

Audience members give the duo an **addition** problem:

What is **263 + 215**?

Leo whispers the **estimate** in Christopher's ear:

300 + 200 = 500

Then, Christopher **breaks it apart** to find the exact sum:

$$263 = 200 + 60 + 3$$
$$215 = 200 + 10 + 5$$
$$400 + 70 + 8 = \textbf{478}!$$

Try this trick at home! (The mouse is optional.)

What is **242 + 536**?

Estimate: _____

242 = _____ + _____ + _____

536 = _____ + _____ + _____

_____ + _____ + _____ = _____

What is **469 + 413**?

Estimate: _____

469 = _____ + _____ + _____

413 = _____ + _____ + _____

_____ + _____ + _____ = _____

What is **385 + 519**?

Estimate: _____

385 = _____ + _____ + _____

519 = _____ + _____ + _____

_____ + _____ + _____ = _____

What is **527 + 266**?

Estimate: _____

527 = _____ + _____ + _____

266 = _____ + _____ + _____

_____ + _____ + _____ = _____

What is **495 + 254**?

Estimate: _____

495 = _____ + _____ + _____

254 = _____ + _____ + _____

_____ + _____ + _____ = _____

There is nothing up Christopher's sleeve. He simply **breaks apart** numbers into hundreds, tens, and ones.

A BIG Wedding

The giant is getting married. He asks Tessie the tailor to make him a dapper outfit. She is going to need more material.

Round each measurement to the nearest ten and hundred.

Hat: 363 ft

nearest ten _____   nearest hundred _____

Necktie: 402 ft

nearest ten _____   nearest hundred _____

Belt: 572 ft

nearest ten _____   nearest hundred _____

Pant leg: 949 ft

nearest ten _____   nearest hundred _____

Sleeve: 762 ft

nearest ten _____   nearest hundred _____

The giant asks the florist for a 135-pound boutonnière. He will wear the fancy flower in a buttonhole.

nearest ten _____

To round to the nearest ten, look at the ones digit. If the ones digit is 5 or more, increase the tens digit by one. 75, 76, 77, 78, and 79 can be rounded up to 80.

Number
and
Operations–
Fractions

Share and Share Alike!

Three brothers want to share 2 sandwiches equally. **Draw lines to divide the second sandwich into** 3 equal parts.

Each brother gets 1 equal part from each sandwich.
So, each brother gets 2 of 6 equal parts, or 2 sixths of the sandwiches.

Four sisters share 3 pies equally. **Draw lines to divide each pie into** 4 equal parts.

Each sister gets **1 equal part** from each pie.

So, each sister gets [   ] of [   ] equal parts, or [   ] **twelfths** of the pies.

Bigfoot Family Picnic

Bigfoot has a big family. So he never takes more than his equal share.

Bigfoot ate one treat.

He ate 1 of **ten equal parts**, or $\frac{1}{10}$.

Bigfoot shared a blanket with three cousins.

He sat on ⬜ of ⬜ equal parts.

Complete the fraction.

$\frac{1}{⬜}$ equal parts

Bigfoot ate cake with his cousins. Shade one part.

He ate ⬜ of ⬜ equal parts.

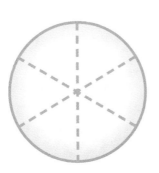

Write a fraction.

$\frac{⬜}{⬜}$ equal parts

Bigfoot went tubing with his favorite cousin Fiona.

Shade one part. He sat on ⬜ of ⬜ equal parts.

Write a fraction.

$\frac{⬜}{⬜}$ equal parts

A **fraction** is a number. The bottom number tells you how many equal parts there are. The top number tells you how many parts you get!

WINNER, WINNER, Chicken Dinner!

Step up and claim your prize!
Evan has 9 prize tickets. He wants a C.A.T. robot.

A robot is $\frac{1}{3}$ of his tickets. How many tickets is it?

Circle 3 equal groups.

Now count the tickets in one group.

$\frac{1}{3}$ of 9 is _____ tickets

Gracie wants a sparkle ring. She has 8 prize tickets.

A ring is $\frac{1}{4}$ of her tickets.

Circle 4 equal groups.

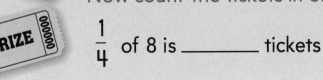

Now count the tickets in one group.

$\frac{1}{4}$ of 8 is _____ tickets

Ruby has 8 tickets, too. She wants a red light bulb.

A bulb is $\frac{3}{4}$ of her tickets.

Draw 8 tickets. Circle 4 equal groups.

Now count the tickets in three groups. $\frac{3}{4}$ of 8 is _____ tickets

Isaac has 18 tickets! He wants the chicken dinner. A chicken dinner is $\frac{1}{2}$ of his tickets. Draw 18 tickets. Circle 2 equal groups.

Now count the tickets in one group.

$\frac{1}{2}$ of 18 is _____ tickets

Furry Friends

Everyone brings a pet to the Furry Friends parade.

There are 3 chihuahuas. One fourth of the dogs are chihuahuas.

How many dogs are in the parade?

$\frac{1}{4}$ tells you that there are four equal groups of dogs.

There are 3 chihuahuas in the first group. Draw 3 dogs in each remaining group.

Count all the dogs. There are _____ dogs in the parade.

One eighth of the guinea pigs are orange.
There are 3 orange guinea pigs.

How many guinea pigs are in the parade?
$\frac{1}{8}$ tells you that there are eight equal groups of guinea pigs.

Draw remaining groups. There are an equal number of guinea pigs in each group.

There are _____ guinea pigs in the parade.

Eek! Two monkeys stole a baby's banana!
One third of the monkeys have a banana.
How many monkeys are in the parade?

Draw remaining groups.

There are _____
monkeys in the parade.

Orange you glad you left your banana at home?

Slow Going

The turtles raced. Nobody won. How far did each turtle go?

Claude crawled $\frac{2}{4}$ of the way to the finish line.

Label the racecourse. Then circle where he stopped.

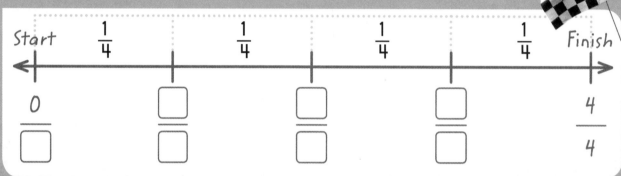

Chance crawled $\frac{1}{3}$ of the way to the finish line.

Label the racecourse. Then circle where he stopped.

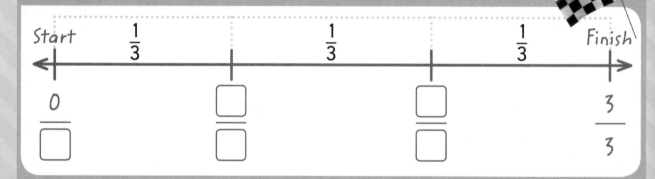

Gunther only had $\frac{1}{4}$ left to go! Circle where he stopped.

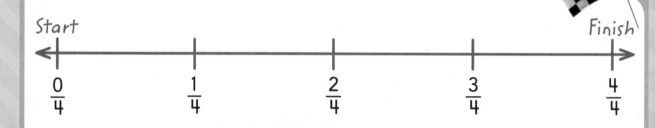

Whack!

The piñata burst! An equal number of each candy fell out.

Rocko grabbed $\frac{2}{3}$ of the taffy. Cass grabbed $\frac{2}{4}$ of the peppermints.

Use the fraction strips to see who got more candy.

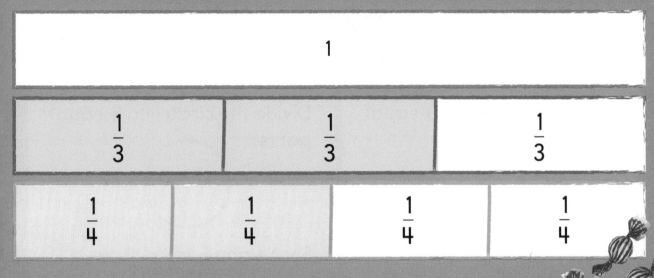

1

| $\frac{1}{3}$ | $\frac{1}{3}$ | $\frac{1}{3}$ |

| $\frac{1}{4}$ | $\frac{1}{4}$ | $\frac{1}{4}$ | $\frac{1}{4}$ |

_____ got more candy!

Lee grabbed $\frac{4}{6}$ of the lollipops. Silas grabbed $\frac{4}{8}$ of the peppermints.

Label the fraction strips. Then color them in to compare fractions.

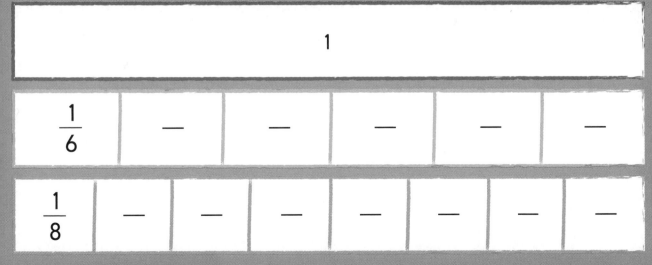

1

| $\frac{1}{6}$ | — | — | — | — | — |

| $\frac{1}{8}$ | — | — | — | — | — | — | — |

_____ got more candy!

Monster Pie

Mel makes a monster pie. $\frac{1}{3}$ of the pie has mealworms. $\frac{1}{4}$ of the pie has slugs. Does the pie have more mealworms or slugs? Draw two circles to compare.

$\frac{1}{3}$ has mealworms

Divide the circle into **3 equal parts.**

Shade one part to show $\frac{1}{3}$.

$\frac{1}{4}$ has slugs

Divide the circle into **4 equal parts.**

Shade one part to show $\frac{1}{4}$.

Compare the shaded parts. $\frac{1}{3}$ is larger than $\frac{1}{4}$. So, $\frac{1}{3}$ $\frac{1}{4}$.

Mel makes a new pie. $\frac{2}{6}$ has stink bugs. $\frac{1}{6}$ has grubs. Draw two circles to compare.

$\frac{2}{6}$ has stink bugs

$\frac{1}{6}$ has grubs

Use < or > to compare the fractions. $\frac{2}{6}$ $\frac{1}{6}$

Mel makes a smoothie. $\frac{2}{3}$ has swamp muck. $\frac{2}{4}$ has green papaya.

Draw two circles to compare.

$\frac{2}{3}$ has swamp muck	$\frac{2}{4}$ has green papaya

Use < or > to compare the fractions. $\frac{2}{3}$ ☐ $\frac{2}{4}$

$\frac{2}{3}$ of monsters eat in. $\frac{2}{6}$ of monsters order takeout.

Draw two circles to compare.

$\frac{2}{3}$ eat in	$\frac{2}{6}$ order takeout

Use < or > to compare the fractions. $\frac{2}{3}$ ☐ $\frac{2}{6}$

MONSTER MASH

1 is less than 2. You can write that as:
1 < 2 or 2 > 1. Either way, the sign always "points" to the smaller number.

FAR OUT Pets

Tar buys a new food bowl for her slime wheezer. The old bowl is $\frac{1}{4}$ full.

Add the same amount to the new bowl. Then write the equivalent fraction.

$$\frac{1}{4} = \frac{\boxed{}}{8}$$

Tar buys new food bowls for her lavender sneeze bobs. The old bowls are $\frac{4}{2}$ full.

Add the same amount to the new bowls. Then write the equivalent fraction.

$$\frac{4}{2} = \frac{\boxed{}}{8}$$

Tar buys a new feeder for her fizzy slugs. The old feeder is $\frac{3}{4}$ full.

Add the same amount to the new feeder. Then write the equivalent fraction.

$$\frac{3}{4} = \frac{6}{\boxed{}}$$

Measurement
and
Data

CAMP WHITEFLY

Time flies at Camp Whitefly!

How much time do campers spend doing each activity?

Start kickball: **9:20**

End kickball: **10:00**

The start time is 9:20.

Skip count by **tens** to count minutes between 9:20 and 10:00.

Trace jumps.

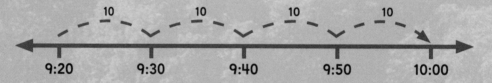

Campers spend _____ minutes playing kickball.

Start pottery: **11:15**

End pottery: **11:45**

Write the missing labels on the number line. Then skip count by **tens** to 11:45.

Campers spend _____ minutes throwing clay.

Canoeing ends at **2:05.** Campers spend **35** minutes on the lake. What time do they start?

The end time is 2:05.

Jump back **5** minutes to the hour. Then jump back **30** more minutes.

Trace jumps.

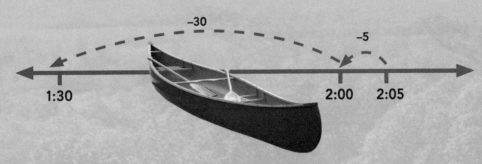

Campers start paddling at _____.

The cookout ends at **1:15.** Campers have **45** minutes to eat. What time does the cookout start?

The cookout starts at _____.

The hotdogs run out **15 minutes after** the cookout starts!

I hope you got there before _____!

Fright Night!

The ghost tracker's watch stops whenever a ghost is near.
Write down each ghostly time.

The **hour hand** points just after the **6**.

The **minute hand** points after **3**.

Count the minutes.

Count 0 at the 12.

Count on by fives: 5, 10, 15.

Then count on by ones: 16, 17, 18.

The ghostly time is **6:18**, or eighteen minutes after six.

It stopped at _____!

It stopped at _____!

It stopped at _____!

It stopped at _____!

DOUBLE TIME

Fred is a safe time traveler. He always enters the time twice on his machine.

Write the time. Then draw hands on the clock.

Fred jumped in the time machine at **3:15 P.M.** He hopped out **55** minutes later at:

_____ A.M. or P.M.

It's **1:55 P.M.** Fred is **35** minutes late for the party! Set the time machine for the party's starting time at:

_____ A.M. or P.M.

Fred goes to bed at **9:00 P.M.** The meteor shower starts **45** minutes after his bedtime. Fred wants to see it! Set the time machine to:

_____ A.M. or P.M.

Fred finished his homework, so he traveled 2000 years into the future! He got back at **7:05 P.M.**, 25 minutes after he left. Fred left at:

_____ A.M. or P.M.

Liter

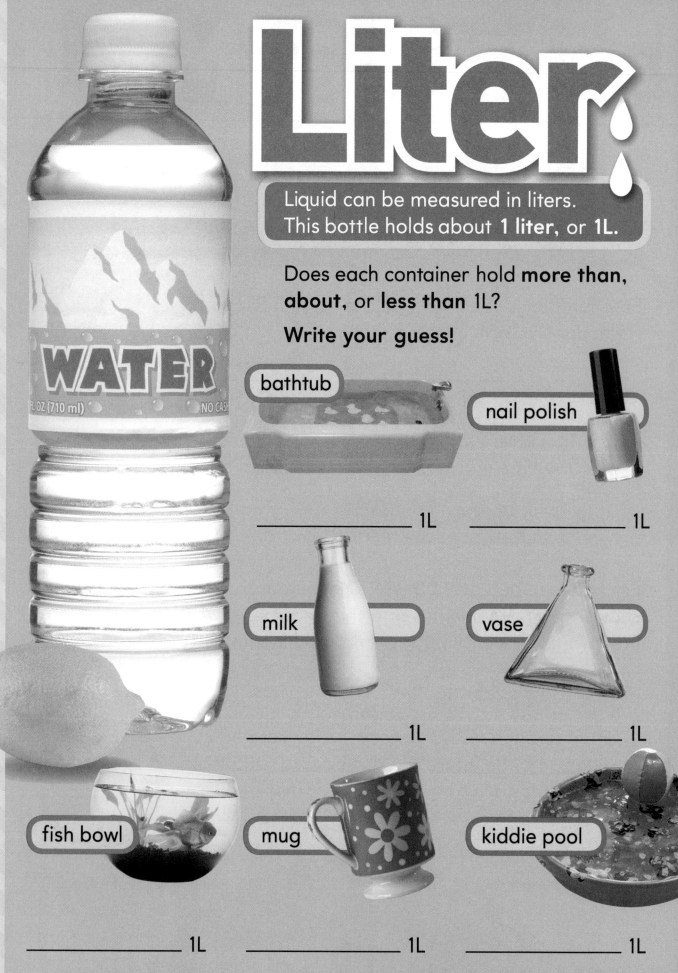

Liquid can be measured in liters. This bottle holds about **1 liter**, or **1L**.

Does each container hold **more than**, **about**, or **less than** 1L?

Write your guess!

bathtub

nail polish

_____ 1L   _____ 1L

milk

vase

_____ 1L   _____ 1L

fish bowl   mug   kiddie pool

_____ 1L   _____ 1L   _____ 1L

WATER

FL OZ (710 ml)   NO CAS

Fling It!

You make a
pocket-sized catapult.
It has a fling power of **1 gram**.

One grape is about **1 gram**. It's just right.
One book is about **1 kilogram**, or 1,000 grapes.
It's too heavy.

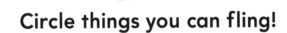

Circle things you can fling!

FIELD AND

The students at Gore Elementary voted for their favorite field day game.

Favorite Game	
Game	**Tally**
Rotten-Egg Relay	卌 II
Brain Toss	卌
Hula Hoop	卌 卌 I
4-Legged Race	卌 IIII

I = 1 vote
卌 = 5 votes

Show the tallies as numbers below.

Favorite Game	
Game	**Tally**
Rotten-Egg Relay	
Brain Toss	
Hula Hoop	
4-Legged Race	9

SCREAM!

The least popular game is

_____.

_____ students like the hula hoop best.

_____ more students chose the rotten-egg relay than the brain toss.

_____ fewer students chose the 4-legged race than the hula hoop.

_____ students chose the brain toss and 4-legged race combined.

This just in!

3 students changed their vote from the hula hoop to the 4-legged race.

Update the numbers in both tables.

Can Do!

The students have a food drive.
They donate canned foods to a local pantry.

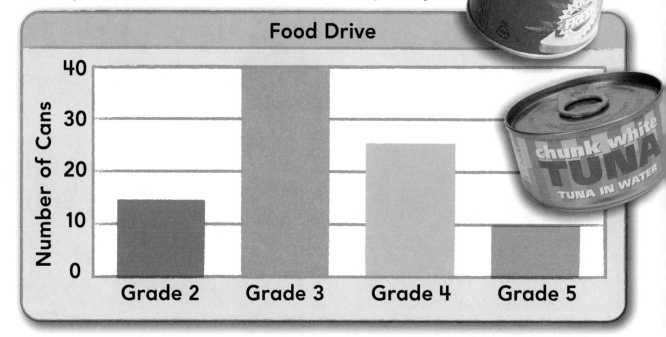

Food Drive

Use the bar graph to answer the questions.

Which grade collected the most cans? _____

How many cans did the grade in second place collect? _____

How many cans were collected in all? _____

Which grade collected 5 fewer cans than Grade 2? _____

Food banks need **non-perishable** foods. Non-perishable foods last a long time. They include canned foods, rice, peanut butter, and cereal.

The students stack food at the pantry.

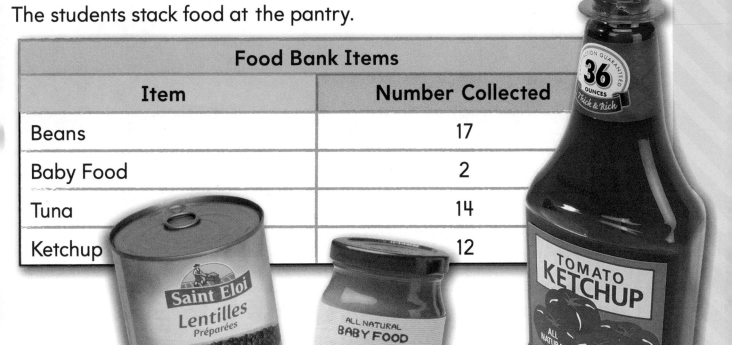

Food Bank Items	
Item	Number Collected
Beans	17
Baby Food	2
Tuna	14
Ketchup	12

Use the data above to draw your own bar graph.

Include a title.

Title: _____

```
18
16
14
12
10
 8
 6
 4
 2
 0
```
____   ____   ____   ____

Kickball Cup

Who tore up the turf at the Kickball Cup?

The picture graph tells the story.

Kickball Scores	
Terrible Twos	⚫⚫⚫⚫⚫
Raging Rainbows	⚫⚫⚫◗
Shark Bites	⚫⚫⚫⚫◖
Blazing Bunnies	⚫⚫⚫⚫⚫⚫⚫
Squid Attack!	⚫⚫⚫⚫⚫

Key: Each ⚫ = 2 points.

How many points is ◖? _____

Which team is in first place? _____

Which teams are tied? _____

How many points did the Shark Bites score? _____

How many fewer points did the Raging Rainbows score than the first place team? _____

A **picture graph** shows information using pictures. A **key** tells you what the picture stands for.

Each team sold T-shirts to fans.

T-Shirts Sold	
Terrible Twos	25
Raging Rainbows	15
Shark Bites	35
Blazing Bunnies	20
Squid Attack!	5

Use the data above to draw your own picture graph.
Include a title. Draw a picture in the key. Each picture equals 5 shirts.

Title:	
Terrible Twos	
Raging Rainbows	
Shark Bites	
Blazing Bunnies	
Squid Attack!	

Key: Each ☐ = 5 shirts.

Choose your favorite team.
Design a T-shirt for them.

Blazing Bunnies
GIVE←BACK

The Blazing Bunnies want to donate the money they made from T-shirt sales.

They ask their fans to choose a charity.

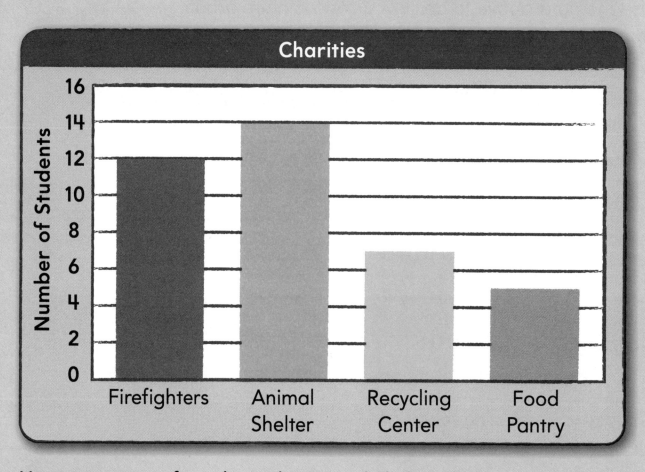

Charities

How many more fans chose the Animal Shelter than the Food Pantry?

_____ more fans. Or, 14 − 5 = [ ]

How many fewer fans chose the Firefighters than the Animal Shelter.

_____ fewer fans. Or, 14 − 12 = [ ]

Did more fans choose the Animal Shelter or the Recycling Center and Food Pantry combined?

[ ] chose the Animal Shelter

[ ] chose the Recycling Center + [ ] chose the Food Pantry

More fans chose:

Animal Shelter

Recycling Center and Food Pantry

The Blazing Bunnies write a check to the Animal Shelter.

They sold **20** T-shirts for **$5** each. In all, they donate $_____.

Write this amount on the check in two ways.

Blazing Bunnies   Date _____

Animal Shelter _____ $ [   ]

_____   Dollars

_____

CARROT STICKS

Blazing Bunny fans call themselves Carrot Sticks. They traveled many miles to the Kickball Cup.

Each X stands for 1 Carrot Stick.

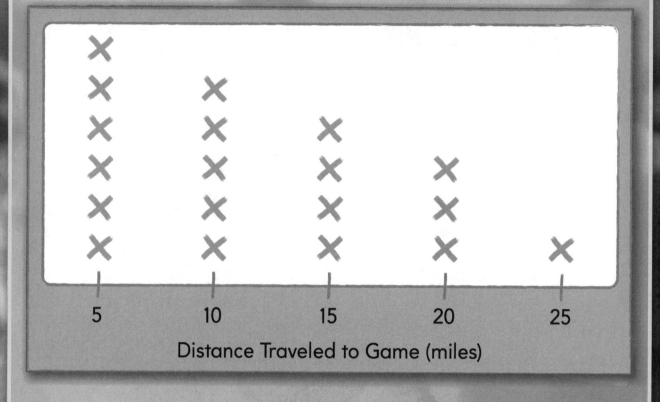

Distance Traveled to Game (miles)

_____ Carrot Sticks went to the game.

Most Carrot Sticks traveled _____ miles to the game.

_____ Carrot Sticks traveled more than 10 miles to the game.

The Carrot Stick that lives the farthest away is

named _____.

A **line plot** uses marks to record each piece of data above a number line!

DRAGON PARENTING

Your dragon will start to breathe fire when the tail is between 2 to 3 inches long.

Measure the tails to the nearest half inch.

Circle the fire-breathers.

_____ inches

_____ inches

_____ inches

_____ inches

There's an inch ruler on page 319.

Rabbit Army

Mason builds rafts for his rabbit army. What is the area of each raft?

Count the number of unit squares to find the area.

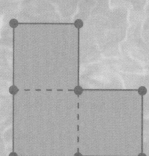

area = _____ square units

Draw lines to show each unit square. **Count to find the area.**

area = _____ square units

area = _____ square units

area = _____ square units

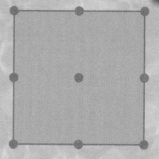

area = _____ square units

Each rabbit takes up one square unit.

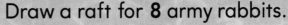

Draw a raft for **6** army rabbits.

Draw a raft for **8** army rabbits.

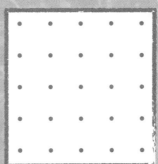

Draw a raft for **6** army rabbits with **6** sides.

Draw a raft for **12** army rabbits with **8** sides.

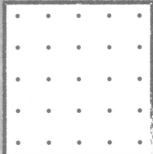

Mason painted some of this raft before lunch.
What is the area that he has left to paint?

There are _____ square units left to paint.

The **area** is the number of unit squares needed to cover a surface. In winter, I use a blanket with a big area. I don't want my tube feet to stick out!

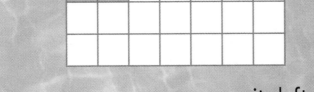

Sunshine SCOUTS

The Sunshine Scouts need 20 square meters to plant pink roses. They don't have all day to count! So they multiply to find the area.

Trace the line to break apart the shape into two rectangles.

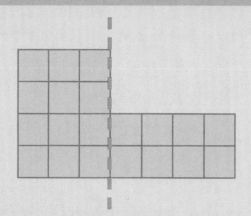

Then multiply and add to find the area.

rectangle 1: ___3___ × ___4___

rectangle 2: _____ × _____

_____ + _____ = _____ square meters

Where should the scouts plant these flowers?

Pink phlox

22 square meters

Hibiscus

10 square meters

Sunflower

24 square meters

Cowboy rose

12 square meters

Draw a line to break apart each shape into rectangles.
Then find the area. Where did the scouts plant each flower?

Flower: _____

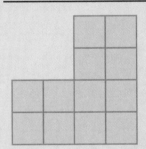

rectangle 1: _____ × _____

rectangle 2: _____ × _____

_____ + _____ =

_____ square meters

Flower: _____

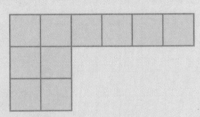

rectangle 1: _____ × _____

rectangle 2: _____ × _____

_____ + _____ =

_____ square meters

Flower: _____

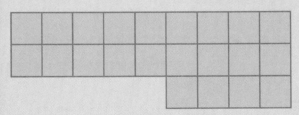

Flower: _____

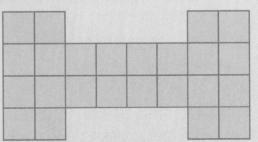

Zombie Tag

To survive Zombie Tag, you draw a **perimeter** around safe zones with silly string. Do you have enough silly string?

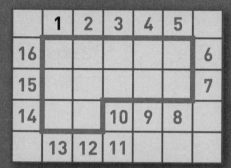

Count each unit around the shape.

The **perimeter** is 16 units.

You need _____ units of silly string.

How much string do you need to protect these zones?

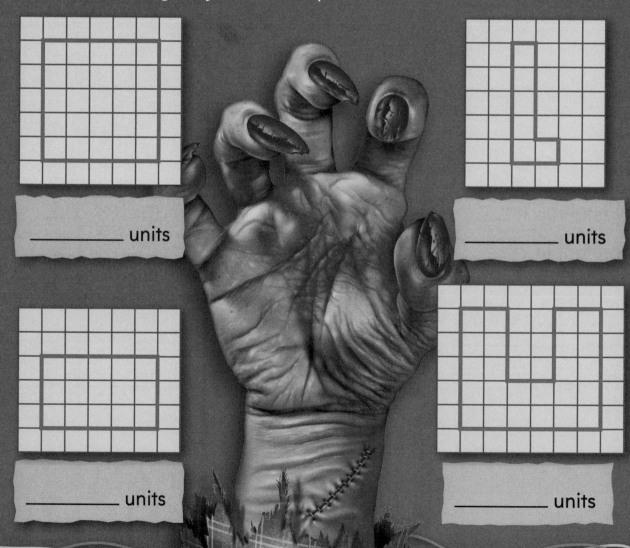

_____ units

_____ units

_____ units

_____ units

Draw safe zones for each perimeter.

16 units

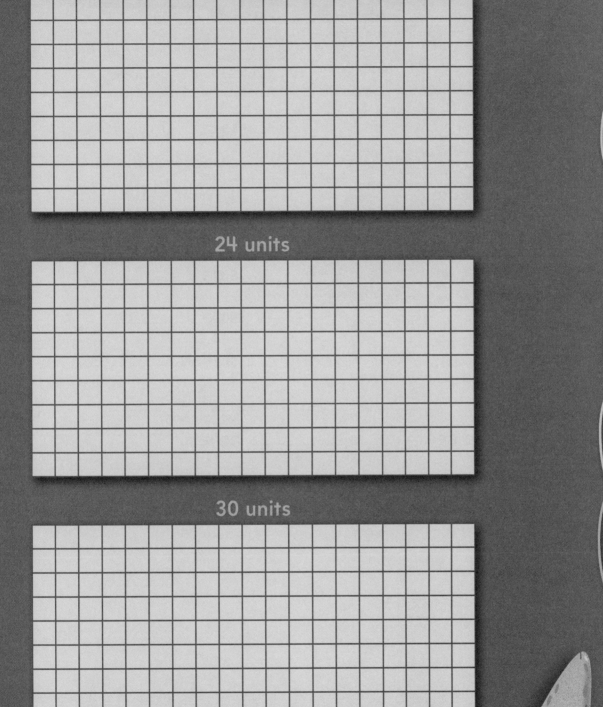

24 units

30 units

The **perimeter** is the distance around a shape.

Sea Glass SALE!

Sadie sells sea glass by the seashore! The customers want to know the **perimeter** of each piece.

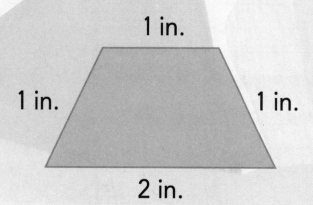

1 in.

1 in.   1 in.

2 in.

Measure the length of each side.
Then add them up.

side 1: _____

side 2: _____

side 3: _____

side 4: _____

_____ + _____ + _____ + _____ = _____

So, the perimeter is _____ inches

Use an inch ruler to find the perimeter of these shapes.

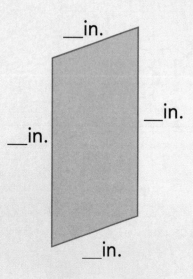

_in.

_in.   _in.

_in.

_____ inches

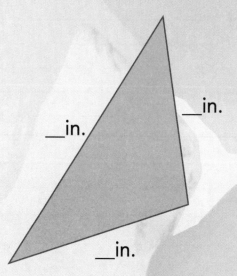

_in.   _in.

_in.

_in.

_____ inches

Use a centimeter ruler to find the perimeter of these shapes.

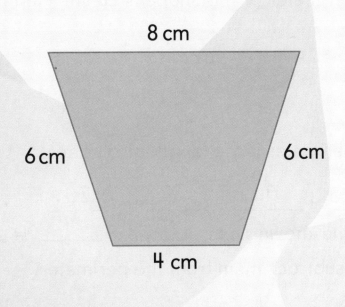

8 cm

6 cm   6 cm

4 cm

_____ centimeters

___cm

___cm

___cm   ___cm

___cm

_____ centimeters

There's an inch ruler on page 319. Flip the ruler to measure in centimeters.

Sadie measured the perimeter of these shapes, but forgot to label one side.

The perimeter of this shape is **20** cm. Find the length of side *a*.

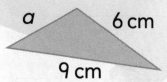

a   6 cm

9 cm

The perimeter is the length of all sides.

$$\underline{\quad 6 \quad} + \underline{\quad 9 \quad} + \underline{\quad a \quad} = \underline{\quad 20 \quad}$$

Add the known sides: $\underline{\quad 6 \quad} + \underline{\quad 9 \quad} = \underline{\quad\quad}$

Then subtract them from the perimeter.

$$\underline{\quad 20 \quad} - \underline{\quad\quad} = \underline{\quad\quad}$$

So, side *a* is _____ centimeters.

These are not for sale! Find the unknown lengths of Sadie's priceless sea glass.

Perimeter = 33 centimeters   Perimeter = 92 inches

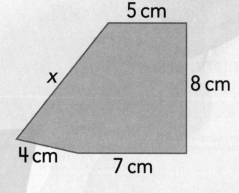

5 cm

x

8 cm

4 cm   7 cm

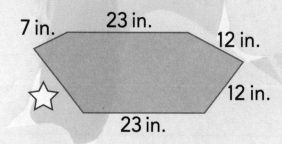

7 in.   23 in.

12 in.

12 in.

23 in.

x = _____ centimeters   ☆ = _____ inches

Geometry

Three witnesses saw a shifty shape.
Can each shape be drawn? Circle the answer.

A Shifty SHAPE!

Merv saw a ray with two endpoints.

possible   **impossible**

Marta saw a closed shape with 6 line segments.

possible   **impossible**

Luke saw an open triangle.

possible   **impossible**

Only one witness saw a possible shape. Draw the shifty shape.

A ray has 1 endpoint and continues in one direction.

An open shape does not start and end at the same point.

A closed shape starts and ends at the same point.

The Right Field

Austin wants to design a new baseball field. **Look at each shape.**

Write how many of each type of angle the shape has.

4	right
0	less than right
0	greater than right

	right
	less than right
	greater than right

	right
	less than right
	greater than right

	right
	less than right
	greater than right

	right
	less than right
	greater than right

	right
	less than right
	greater than right

A **right angle** forms a square corner.

Plane Food

The polygon chef makes plane food.
Today's special is polygon pasta.

Write the name of each shape described on the menu.

3 sides	4 sides	5 sides
3 angles	4 angles	5 angles
_____	_____	_____

6 sides	8 sides	10 sides
6 angles	8 angles	10 angles
_____	_____	_____

decagon

hexagon

octagon

pentagon

quadrilateral

triangle

A **plane shape** is flat. A **polygon** is a plane shape with 3 or more straight sides and angles.

Look at the dashed sides on the polygon pasta.

If they appear to be **parallel**, trace them in red.
If they appear to be **perpendicular**, trace them in green.

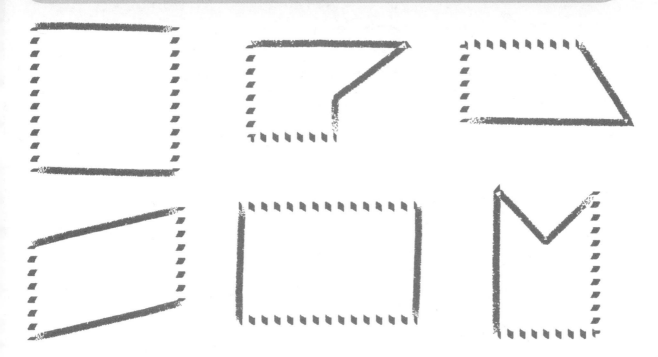

The chef wants to add more polygons to the menu.
Circle polygon shapes.

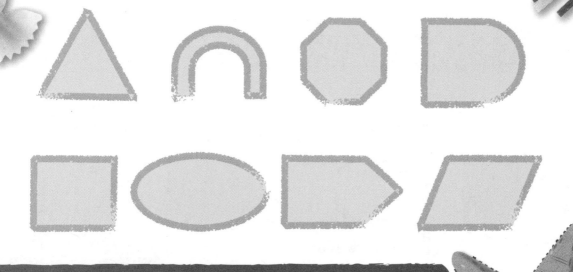

Parallel lines never cross. **Perpendicular lines** do.
They make a right angle where they cross.

Kid
Quadrilateral!

A wizard turned the kids on Square Place into quadrilaterals!

Reverse the spell.

Write the name of each kid next to the matching shape.

Skylar has 2 pairs of opposite sides that are parallel, 4 sides that are of equal length and 4 right angles.

Rhys has 2 pairs of opposite sides that are parallel and 4 sides that are of equal length.

Hector has 2 pairs of opposite sides that are parallel, 2 pairs of sides that are of equal length and 4 right angles.

Trixie has 1 pair of opposite sides that are parallel and none of her sides are of equal length.

It's _____! It's _____! It's _____! It's _____!

You find the wizard's spell book.
Now you can make quadrilaterals!

Connect four endpoints to make a square.

Then say, **Quad-roosh!**

Connect four endpoints to make a
trapezoid, like Trixie!

Then say, **Quad-roosh!**

ACUTE NECKLACE!

Write the triangle's letter under each bucket that describes it. Each triangle can go into two buckets. Some go into more!

Help Beryl win the acute necklace!

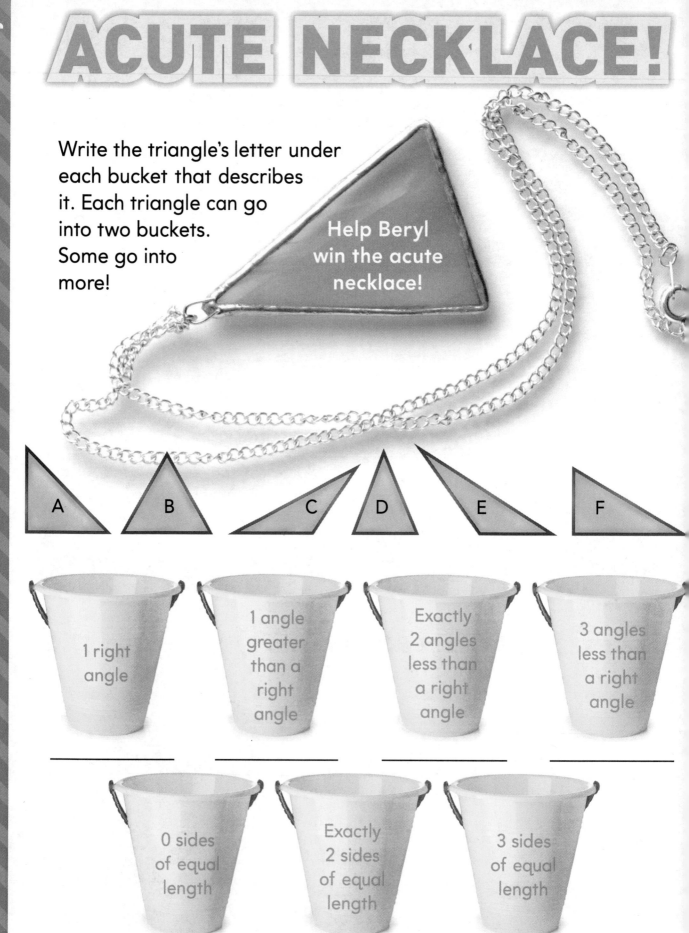

A   B   C   D   E   F

1 right angle

1 angle greater than a right angle

Exactly 2 angles less than a right angle

3 angles less than a right angle

0 sides of equal length

Exactly 2 sides of equal length

3 sides of equal length

Nature of Science

SUPERVISION

Scientists use tools to help them see tiny and tinier creatures.
Draw a line from the picture to the tool used to see it.

weevil

butterfly

microscope

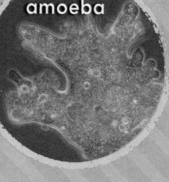

amoeba

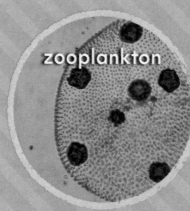

zooplankton

hand lens

Look in your refrigerator. Pick something to "see."
Draw it two ways.

Using just your eyes

Using a hand lens

236

YOU the Zoologist

Look at the turtle. Get close! What can you infer by looking at it? Write your inferences.

hard shell

sharp toenails

webbed feet

Inferences: help it dig   help it swim   protects it

When you **observe**, you tell what you see. *The shell has a wavy pattern. Like water!* When you **infer**, you offer an explanation for what you see. *The wavy pattern might help the turtle hide in water.*

Sink or Float?

Did you ever wonder why some things sink or float? Then you are thinking like a scientist. Circle the floating objects.

Why do you think they float? Write your guess.

_____

_____

Predict! Circle items that you think will float.
Make an X on those you think will sink.

Now fill a glass with water. Add each item. **Does it sink or float?**

	It sinks!	It floats!
penny	☐	☐
bottle cap	☐	☐
ice cube	☐	☐
egg	☐	☐
crayon	☐	☐
rock	☐	☐

When you **predict**, you guess what will happen based on what you already know.

Get to Sleep!

You need 10 to 11 hours of sleep each night. How many hours do you sleep? Keep a sleep log for one week.

Hours of Sleep

	Went to sleep	Woke up	Total hours slept
Sunday			
Monday			
Tuesday			
Wednesday			
Thursday			
Friday			
Saturday			

You can show your sleep data in a line graph. For each day, draw a line across to the number of hours you slept.

Sunday shows 4 hours of sleep. If you slept more than that, make the line longer.

Hours of Sleep

	0	1	2	3	4	5	6	7	8	9	10	11	12
Sunday													
Monday													
Tuesday													
Wednesday													
Thursday													
Friday													
Saturday													

You keep data in a sleep log. When you sleep *like* a log, you are probably having a nice dream about circus monkeys and popcorn.

A Million Maps!

A map can tell you how to get from one place to another. When the president invites you to dinner, you will need a map to get to his house.

Find a mapping tool on the Internet.

Get directions to the White House. **How far is it from your home?**

[ ] miles   [ ] hours   [ ] minutes

The map below does not give directions. It shows _____.
(Underline one.)

rainfall   climate   landforms

World Climates

ARCTIC OCEAN

NORTH AMERICA   EUROPE   ASIA

PACIFIC OCEAN   ATLANTIC OCEAN   AFRICA   PACIFIC OCEAN

Equator   Equator

SOUTH AMERICA   INDIAN OCEAN

AUSTRALIA

KEY
- Temperate
- Tropical
- Arctic

N NE NW W E SW SE S

ANTARCTICA

Draw a line from the animal to a region.

The red robin lives in a temperate climate.

The macaw lives in a tropical climate.

Leap, Frog!

Frog America wants to publish your photo in the next issue.

Provide a few details to go along with the photo.

Measure the longest front leg.

[ ] centimeters

Measure the longest back leg.

[ ] centimeters

Write the difference between the front and back leg.

[ ] centimeters

Tell one thing about the frog you can measure with these tools.

stopwatch

_____

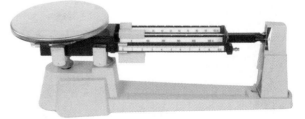

balance

_____

WEATHER WATCHER

You are a substitute meteorologist. Look at the Weather Forecast bar graph. Complete the statements to give the forecast.

WEATHER FORECAST

Temperature F°

95
90
85
80
75
70

 Monday
 Tuesday
 Wednesday
 Thursday
 Friday

Day of week

The temperature on Tuesday will be _____.

The coldest day this week will be _____.

The hottest day this week will be _____.

On Wednesday, we'll see some _____.

Don't leave the house without your _____!

_____, _____, and _____ are cloud-free!

A **meteorologist** is a weather scientist. You can get a weather forecast on your phone, the Internet, TV, or radio.

Problem Solved!

An **engineer** is a scientist who builds something to solve a problem.

Describe the **problem** each thing solved.

Problem: _____

_____

Solution: space food

Problem: _____

_____

Solution: washing machine

Problem: _____

_____

Solution: hair dryer

Read the paragraph. Underline the **problem**. Circle the **solution**.

It is still too dangerous for humans to land on Mars. For one, the radiation is deadly! A Mars rover makes it possible to explore Mars safely.

Better Over Time!

Designs get better over time.
Order these designs from 1 to 3. 1 is the oldest,
3 is the newest.

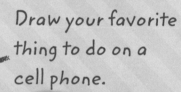

Draw your favorite
thing to do on a
cell phone.

Check the ways the cell phone
got better over time.

- [ ] It got smaller.
- [ ] It got lighter.
- [ ] It can take pictures.
- [ ] It can search the Internet.
- [ ] It can play movies.

Martin Cooper invented the first cell phone
in 1973. It weighed about 2 pounds. That's
the weight of about 8 cells phones today.

TIME to Change!

Look at the technology from each decade. **Suggest how to improve it.**

This camera uses film. After you take 20 pictures, you have to change the roll.

Cool, daddy-o!

You step back to the **1960s**. Tell them to make a camera that

_____

_____

Clickety clack! Don't talk back!

You're in the **1950s**. Tell them to make a computer that

_____

_____

It was a dark and stormy night . . .

People type words onto paper. There is no delete key on a typewriter. It is not easy to edit your work.

Radical! You're in the **1980s**. Tell them to make a phone that

_____

_____

Phones like this are connected to the wall.

Like Clockwork!

Over 4,000 fluorescent bulbs keep the station bright.

Every day, 750,000 people pass through Grand Central Terminal. Technologies, such as the **train schedule board** and **lighting**, keep the terminal in action.

Circle other examples of technology.

shoes   windows

sunlight   suitcases

people   coats

umbrellas

A train schedule board tells when trains depart, and from which track.

Technology doesn't have to plug in. It is anything people make or do to change the natural world, from stairs to candy wrappers.

Life
Science

A Plant's Life

Plant Quarterly asks you to tell the story of a tomato plant's life as an information graphic.

Find and underline the four stages in a tomato plant's life cycle.

Plants go through many stages in their lives. These stages form a cycle, or pattern, that repeats again and again.

A tomato plant comes from a seed. When the seed is watered, it germinates, or breaks open. A small plant, or seedling, grows out of it. The plant grows into an adult, which makes flowers. The flowers fall off the plant, and the plant makes fruit. The fruit holds new seeds. The cycle repeats!

Now complete the information graphic.

Draw it!

Title: _____

Stage:

Description:

This seed will grow into a large tomato plant.

Stage:

Description:

When a seed is watered, it begins to germinate.

A tiny new plant comes out of the seed.

Draw it!

Stage: Adult Plant

Description:

_____

_____

_____

Stage: Fruit

Description:

_____

_____

_____

In a tomato plant, the fruit holds the seeds. In other flowering plants, the flowers hold the seeds. A pine tree stores its seeds in cones!

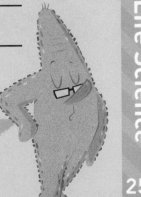

Big Job,
Little Insect

Pollen is a yellow, powdery material that helps plants reproduce. Birds, insects, and even the wind move pollen.

> Circle the pictures that show pollen being moved.
> Star the pictures that show seeds being moved.

Pollen sticks to the insect's legs. That's how the insect moves pollen from one plant to another. A *pollinated* plant can make seeds. Seeds grow into new plants.

Pretty SWEET!

A **producer** is a living thing that makes its own food. *Inside* of itself!

A plant uses sunlight to change water and carbon dioxide, a gas in the air, into sugars.

The tomato plant looks hungry! **Draw three things it needs to make sugars.**

Circle the plant part where food is made. Hint: There are at least 20 on this plant.

The process used to make food is called photosynthesis (foht-oh-SIHN-thuh-sis). Plants give off oxygen when they make food. And we breathe it!

Protect the PREY!

An animal that hunts other animals for food is a **predator**. An animal that is hunted for food is called **prey**.

Look at each pair. Circle the prey to protect it.

I am a predator and prey. I hunt and eat mussels and oysters. But, crabs and gulls hunt and eat me. It's not my favorite subject to talk about.

Baby, It's YOU!

Draw a line from an early life cycle stage to a later stage.

pupa

egg

ladybug

cub

chick

lion

A butterfly, like most insects, has a major change in its body form as it grows. It's called metamorphosis (met-uh-MAWR-fuh-sis).

Draw the last stage of this butterfly's metamorphosis.

You did not go through **metamorphosis**. From the start, you looked like a small version of your parents.

Staying ALIVE

1	**2**	**3**
Stripes warn birds that it is not tasty.	A hooked beak helps it tear meat from its prey.	Its color helps it hide from predators.

I think I learned something. If a predator can't *see* me, then it can't *eat* me. That's called **camouflage** (KAM-uh-flazh). I just need to find a sand-colored jumpsuit.

An adaptation helps animals survive where they live. Match each adaptation to the animal with that trait. Write the number.

4	5	6
Long ears help it keep cool in the desert.	A large nose helps it detect if food is safe to eat.	Powerful jaws help it grip its food.

This butterfly wants to scare you off.

It **mimics** an _____.

Get Buggy!

900,000 living insects are known. Scientists believe that the same number (if not more) have yet to be named.

Who will find and name them? **Maybe *you*!**

Choose one or more insect orders to study. Circle them.

Coleoptera   Diptera   Hymenoptera   Blattodea

Lepidoptera   Odonata   Orthoptera

Charles Henry Turner was an **entomologist**, a scientist who studies insects. In 1910, he proved that honeybees can see color. The next year, he proved they can also see patterns. Turner found that some ants move in circles toward their home. To honor his work, other scientists call this behavior "Turner's circling."

Draw a path that shows "Turner's circling."

An **adult mayfly** lives for 24 hours. A **termite** queen can rule for 50 years!

Ecosystem

Match each living thing to an ecosystem. Draw a line.

cactus

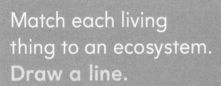
toucan

mountain lion

blue whale

prairie dog

rainforest ecosystem

ocean ecosystem

desert ecosystem

grassland ecosystem

mountain ecosystem

Wildfire

A fire burned through the forest. Complete the story to tell the effects. **Circle the correct words.**

The fire was caused by (**a natural event/people**). Lightning struck a tree. After that, the fire spread (**slowly/fast**). In less than one hour, it (**planted/destroyed**) thousands of trees. A coyote left the fire-burned area to find a new (**habitat/food chain**). Animals that stayed will have to compete for (**crops/resources**).

The fire was damaging, but it cleared space for new plant growth. Ashes from burned plants added (**nutrients/sunlight**) to the soil. And pinecones, heated by the fire, opened to release (**seeds/flowers**). After a time, new and different (**plants/animals**) will grow. The ecosystem will change.

A fire can change an ecosystem.

Name two other events that can change an ecosystem.

_____   _____

If the plant life changed after the fire, the coyote may never move back. *Why?* A coyote eats rabbits. But the rabbits may not return to eat the new plants.

Earth
and
Space Science

Hike It! Climb It!

The new issue of *Landform Weekly* arrived.
Label each landform. Star the one you would travel to see.

> **valley** Low land between mountains or hills.
>
> **canyon** A valley with steep sides.

Landform: _____   Landform: _____

You decide to visit the Matterhorn, a mountain in the Swiss Alps.

The mountain's surface is _____ and _____.

Circle the right shoes for your climb.

Mountains can be formed by volcanoes or when Earth's crust pushes together.

Not So TOUGH!

Earth's surface can change. Even mountains get smaller as they get older.

Weathering can widen the cracks on this statue.

Order the steps from 1 to 3.

- [ ] The water freezes. Ice forms in the cracks. The ice takes up more space than the water did.

- [ ] Water moves into cracks and stays there.

- [ ] The ice widens the cracks. Pieces of rock may break off.

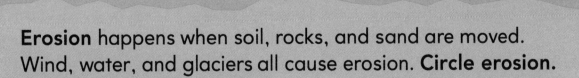

Erosion happens when soil, rocks, and sand are moved. Wind, water, and glaciers all cause erosion. **Circle erosion.**

Quick Change!

Earth's surface can change in minutes—or even seconds!

Label each picture. Then draw a line to the cause.

earthquake   volcano   flood   landslide

Earth's plates push together, pull apart, or slide past each other. The ground shakes.

Rock underground melts and moves upward. It erupts through the top of a mountain. As it cools and hardens, it changes the shape of the mountain.

Rainwater loosens dirt on the side of a hill or mountain. The dirt slides downhill.

Streams, rivers, and lakes fill with rainwater and overflow.

Earthquakes and volcanoes are caused by the same thing – movements of the Earth's crust.

Minor Tremor, OUTSTANDING SHAKE

There can be as many as 10 earthquakes a day in the U.S. *Did you feel any?*

The strongest earthquake measures _____ on the scale.

Any earthquake that measures _____ or higher is noteworthy or stronger.

An earthquake measures 1 on the scale. Emergency crews won't be needed because it is _____.

To be _____, an earthquake must measure 8 on the scale.

Any earthquake that measures _____ or lower is minor to insignificant.

When's the next *big one*?

Seismologists study earthquakes, but they don't have a reliable way to predict them.

Some people think that toads can predict earthquakes. Days before an earthquake occurred in L'Aquila, Italy, the toads ran away!

Earthquake Magnitude Scale (1–10)

10	Extraordinary
9	Outstanding
8	Far-reaching
7	High
6	Noteworthy
5	Intermediate
4	Moderate
3	Minor
2	Low
1	Insignificant

A **Richter scale** tells how much energy is released during an earthquake. Most earthquakes measure below 3 on the scale. People don't feel these *microquakes*.

It's Natural

A **natural resource** is something people can use that comes from nature. **Circle them.**

potato

wind

Granola Bar
granola bar

coal

toothpaste

wood

gum

Choose three natural resources. Write how you use them.

_____wood_____ is made into _____a pencil_____

_____ is made into _____

_____ is made into _____

_____ is made into _____

A **renewable** resource can be replaced easily. A **nonrenewable** resource cannot. It will eventually run out.

Is it renewable or nonrenewable? **Make an X.**

Resource	Renewable	Nonrenewable
Sun	x	
Oil		
Natural gas		
Wind		
Corn		
Water		
Diamond		
Trees		
Coal		

Coal is burned to produce electricity. Coal is a **fossil fuel**.

It took (hundreds/thousands/millions) of years to form.

Most **nonrenewable** resources are dug up from the ground. It's important to **conserve** them. One way is to turn off the lights when you leave a room.

What Goes Around

Recycle! Draw a line from each object, through the correct bin, to the object it becomes.

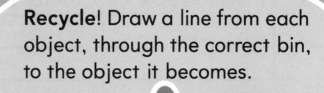

PAPER METAL PLASTIC GLASS

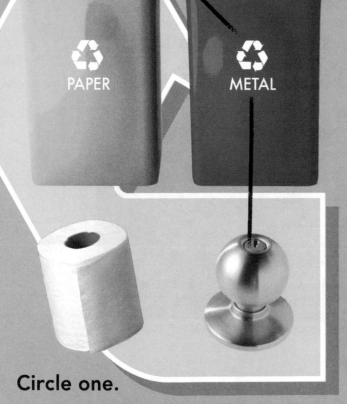

Circle one.

Recycling keeps (thousands/millions/billions) of pounds of material from being thrown in the trash.

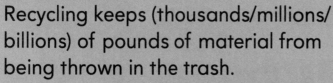

Grow This!

Local farmers test the pH of the soil in their fields. Tell them what to grow.

pH Scale

| 3 | | | | 7 | | | 10 |

Recommend two crops to each farmer.

_____

_____

_____

_____

_____

_____

Garlic grows best in soil that has a pH around 8.

Blueberries grow best in soil that has a pH around 4.

Broccoli grows best in soil that has a pH around 6.

Radishes grow best in soil that has a pH around 4.

Asparagus grows best in soil that has a pH around 8.

Carrots grow best in soil that has a pH around 6.

Presto Change-O!

When water **evaporates**, it changes from a liquid to a gas, or *water vapor*.

When it **condenses**, water vapor changes back to liquid water.

Tell what is happening to water in each picture. Label it **evaporation** or **condensation.**

When water vapor touches the cold glass, it loses heat. It changes into droplets on the glass.

The bison's breath has water vapor. When it mixes with cool air, it changes into droplets of water that look like a cloud.

The sun heats the puddle. It will change to water vapor and disappear.

After a cool night, water vapor forms water droplets, called dew, on the grass.

Water is always on the move.
Label three parts of the water cycle.

evaporation   condensation   precipitation

_____

_____

_____

The sun heats the ocean. Water **evaporates** to water vapor.
The vapor cools. It **condenses** to water droplets in clouds. It
can fall to Earth as **precipitation**—rain, snow, or hail.

HIGH TIDE, LOW TIDE

The moon's gravity pulls on the ocean. When the moon is above an ocean, the water rises. On the other side of Earth, water also rises. The water in between falls.

Ocean water rises at **high tide** and falls at **low tide**. Which tide does the picture show? **Circle one.**

low tide   high tide

The moon (can/cannot) be directly above this beach.

A **tide pool** is a shallow pool of water left behind in a rocky area during **low tide**.

Predict what will happen to this tide pool at **high tide**.

_____

_____

_____

_____

Word Twister

Unscramble the words to complete each weather fact.

teerhwa — The condition of the atmosphere at any one place and time is the ___ ___ ___ ___ ___ ___ ___.

peerturame — The ___ ___ ___ ___ ___ ___ ___ ___ ___ ___ ___ is a measure of how hot or cold something is.

zblrziad — A ___ ___ ___ ___ ___ ___ ___ ___ is a snowstorm with strong wind and a very low temperature.

oodrtna — A ___ ___ ___ ___ ___ ___ ___ is a small, spinning column of very strong wind.

rcirneahu — A tropical storm with winds of 119 kilometers (74 miles) per hour or more is a ___ ___ ___ ___ ___ ___ ___ ___ ___.

locud — A ___ ___ ___ ___ ___ shape can tell you what kind of weather may be coming.

sasanK   esTax   eret   rac

Tornadoes are common in states with large plains, such as ___ ___ ___ ___ ___ and ___ ___ ___ ___ ___ ___. Tornado winds are so strong that they can rip a ___ ___ ___ ___ out of the ground and move a ___ ___ ___ through the air.

TURN, TURN!

You got a spacecraft kit for your birthday.
You put it together and zoom up into the stars.
You look down at Earth from above the North Pole.

It is day on the Earth's half that faces the sun.

Draw the sun's location.

Earth's Rotation

The Earth turns in the opposite direction of a clock.

Trace the path that shows how Earth turns.

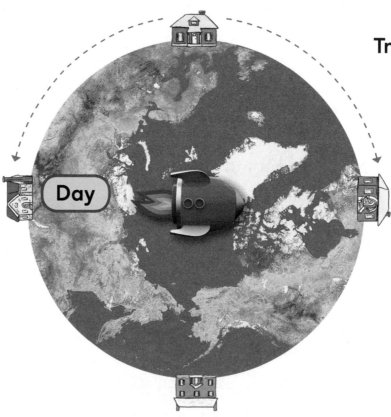

Day

Circle the house where it is **morning**.

Box the house where it is **evening**.

Star the house where it is **night**.

Here's a hint. As the Earth turns, morning becomes day.

Moon Glow

Like Earth, the moon is lit up by the sun. As the moon revolves around Earth, different amounts of its lit side can be seen.

Use the descriptions below to label the moon phases.

The lit side of a **new moon** faces away from Earth. We see no moon at all.

A **first-quarter moon** looks like a half-circle and it is lit on the right side.

We see all of the moon's lit side during a **full moon**.

A **third-quarter moon** looks like a half circle, but it is lit on the left side.

We see **crescent moons** just before and just after a new moon.

Moon Phases

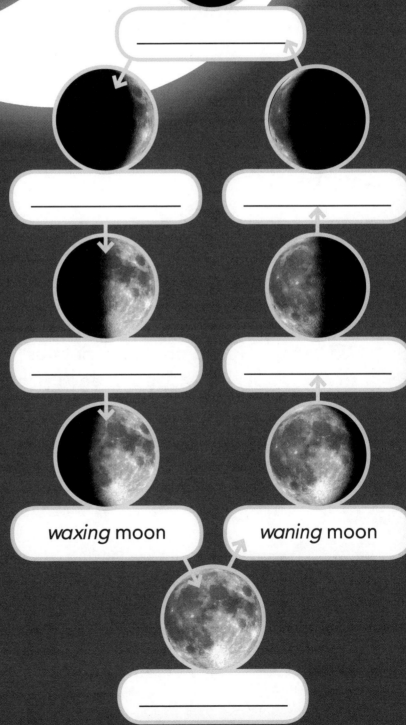

waxing moon

waning moon

Metal Mixer!

A **metallurgist** (met-el-er-jist) is a scientist who works with metals. They also combine metals to make new metals.

 Iron is strong. Mixed with other materials, it becomes steel.

 Aluminum is a light metal. It does not rust.

 Copper is a soft, red metal. It can conduct electricity.

Based on its properties, which metal is likely used in each product?

_____   _____   _____

An **alloy** is a metal that is made by mixing two or more metals. Bronze is made by mixing tin and copper.

Physical Science

TINY Matters!

Tiny the Great Dane is matter. He takes up space. *A lot of space!* **Circle physical properties that describe Tiny.**

soft   big   playful   gray

Write a **physical property** to describe each group.

_____

_____

_____

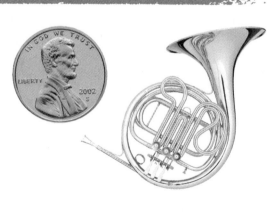

_____

A **physical property** is something you can observe or measure directly, like **size, shape, color**, and **texture**. While greatness can be measured by kindness, it is not a physical property.

Connect the objects in order, from the one with the **least mass** to the one with the **most mass**.

What is the **most massive** object in your home?

_____

Mass is the amount of matter an object has. A smaller object can have more mass than a bigger object. If it is harder to move, it has more mass.

PHYSICAL or CHEMICAL?

Matter can change. Is each change physical or chemical? Write *P* for physical, or *C* for chemical.

Folding, tearing, and cutting are physical changes. In a physical change, the type of matter stays the same. In a chemical change, new kinds of matter are formed. And they likely can't change back!

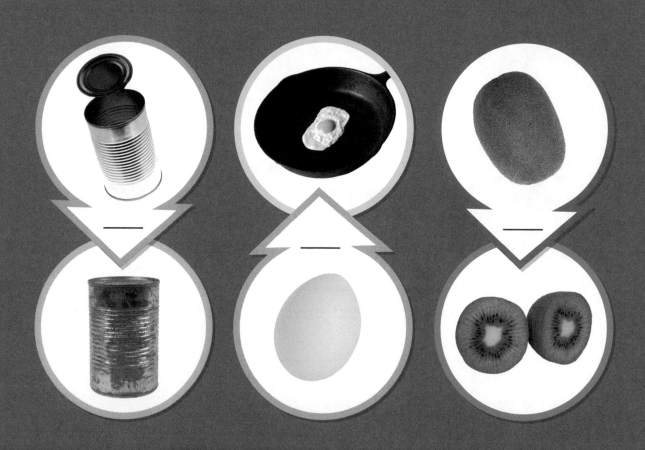

Describe a **physical change** you made or saw today.

_____

_____

Describe a **chemical change** you made or saw today.

_____

_____

Signs of a chemical change include a change in **color, texture**, and **smell**.

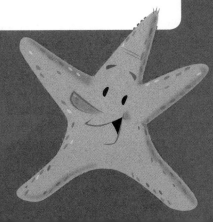

Machine Operator

A simple machine makes work easier.
Match each machine to two examples.

Draw a line.

Lever

A **lever** helps lift things.
It is a bar that turns on
a fixed point called a
fulcrum. The load, or
what you are moving,
is on the end of the lever.

Pulley

A **pulley** can lift
a load straight
up into the air.
It is a wheel with
a rope or chain
around it.

ferris wheel

climbing gear

pencil sharpener

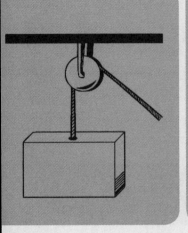

Wheel-and-Axle

A **wheel-and-axle** uses a turning motion to make work easier. The wheel and axle are connected. When you turn a doorknob (the "wheel") the axle turns, too.

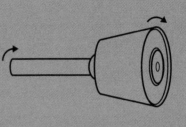

fork

crane

rake

Circle a compound machine.

A **compound machine** is made up of two or more simple machines. Scissors have two levers. I have five—my arms!

Taking Up SPACE

Matter takes up space. How much? **Find the volume.**

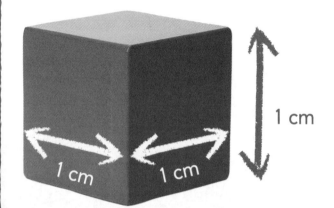

$$\frac{1}{\text{length}} \times \frac{1}{\text{width}} \times \frac{1}{\text{height}} = \underline{\qquad} \text{ cubic centimeter}$$

1 cm
1 cm
1 cm

This cube's volume is one cubic centimeter.

Now find the volume of this cube.

$$\underline{\qquad} \times \underline{\qquad} \times \underline{\qquad} = \underline{\qquad} \text{ cubic centimeters}$$
length   width   height

Check your math. Count the smaller cubes in the larger cube, including the ones you can't see!

I count _____ cubes.

When you climb into a full bathtub, the water rises. The amount the water rises is your **volume!**

Community

Community Clues

You visit this **community**. What do you see?

Write two words to describe the **geography** of this community.

_____

_____

Name three kinds of **jobs** people have in this community.

_____

_____

Name two kinds of **goods** being used in this community.

Hint: Goods are things people make.

_____

_____

Circle people and places in *your* community.

citizens

museum

library

government

store

A **community** is a place where people live, work, and play.

HELP YOUR Neighbor

A good citizen follows the law, pays taxes, and votes. A good citizen can also work with others to solve problems.

Write a caption to describe what these citizens are doing.

_____
_____
_____

_____
_____
_____

_____
_____
_____

_____
_____
_____

Underline how Jimmy Carter is a good citizen.

Jimmy Carter was once President of the United States. He volunteers for Habitat for Humanity, a group that builds homes for people who cannot pay for them.

CHANGE IT

| **bridge** | **building** | **canal** | **dam** |
| a path over something | a place where people work together | a waterway dug across land | a water blockade |

Take a ride 250 feet underwater! The Channel Tunnel, or "Chunnel," is an underwater tunnel between England and France. To build it, British and French workers dug from each side, meeting up in the middle.

England France

People change the land around them to meet their needs.
Label each picture to show some ways.

farm	mine	road	tunnel
land that is cleared to grow crops or raise animals	a deep tunnel or an open pit carved into the land	a flat surface to travel on	a path that runs under something

_____ _____ _____ _____

Star ways that help with transportation.

The Hoover Dam controls the flow of the Colorado River. It holds back millions of gallons of water. Before the dam was built, the river would flood farms.

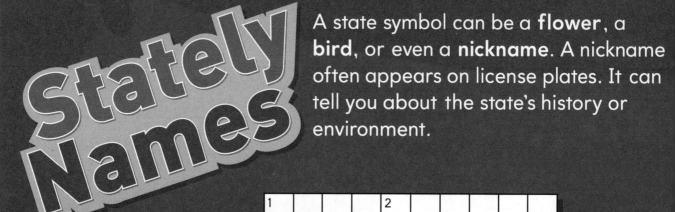

Stately Names

A state symbol can be a **flower**, a **bird**, or even a **nickname**. A nickname often appears on license plates. It can tell you about the state's history or environment.

Across

1. The Golden State

3. Constitution State

7. The First State

8. The Mount Rushmore State

9. The Aloha State

Down

2. The Sunshine State

4. The Cornhusker State

5. The Sunflower State

6. The Bluegrass State

Write your state's nickname. It might have more than one!

Nickname: _____

A state **motto** can also give a clue about the state's history. **Guess the state.**

Eureka means, "I found it!" It refers to the discovery of gold in this state.

— — — — — — — — — —

North to the Future is this northern state's motto.

— — — — — —

Ever Upward is a good motto for this state with tall buildings.

— — — — — — — —

Write your state's motto. What does it mean?

Motto: _____

It means: _____

The bald eagle is the national bird of the U.S. Each state has a bird symbol, too. This popular bird is a symbol of seven states. **Circle it.**

cardinal    turkey    quail

Choose symbols for your family.

Family nickname: _____

Family motto: _____

Family bird: _____

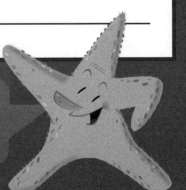

In North Carolina, our motto is "To Be, Rather Than to Seem." That seems to be rather a special motto!

CAPITOL IDEAS!

State **representatives** and **senators** work at the Capitol building in Washington, D.C. They write new laws for people to follow.

Each state sends two senators to the Capitol.
How many senators work at the Capitol? _____ senators

435 representatives work at the Capitol. States with a bigger population, or more people, get more representatives.
Today, California has 53 representatives. Delaware has 1.
Check the reasons this number can change:

☐ California's population goes up

☐ California's population goes down

☐ Delaware's population goes up

Get to work! Representatives work in the Capitol's South wing, or **House**. Senators work in the North wing, or **Senate**.

Label the House **and** Senate.

Hint: The pool is on the west side of the Capitol.

The Capitol building was built in 1793 when there were 15 states. As the United States grew, so did the Capitol building.

Look at the picture. How did the Capitol building change over time?

_____

Look for a clue in the picture. The Statue of Freedom was added after the year _____.

Sep 1860

Senator Nelson, from Wisconsin, founded Earth Day in 1970. On this day, citizens plant trees or pick up trash to protect natural resources.

Choice and
CONSEQUENCE

Campbell has free time. Help him decide what to do.
Describe a possible consequence of each choice.

Skate with friends

or

Volunteer at the animal shelter

A result is:

_____

_____

_____

A result is:

_____

_____

_____

Circle the activity with the best consequence. (There is no right answer!)

| Skate with friends | Volunteer at the animal shelter |

OK for OKLAHOMA!

It's Oklahoma Day at school! The students wear Oklahoma colors green and white. Wyatt sings the song *Oklahoma!* Wendy makes a timeline.

Oklahoma Early History

| 1800 | 1850 | 1900 | 1925 |

1803 As part of the Louisiana Purchase, the United States buys Oklahoma, but not the Panhandle.

1819 Oklahoma is made part of the Arkansas Territory.

1830 The Five Tribes begin to move to Oklahoma.

1890 Congress establishes the Oklahoma Territory and adds the Panhandle region.

Oklahoma becomes a state in 1907. Add this event to the timeline. **Make a dot. Then write a description.**

Circle the part of the state not included in the Louisiana Purchase.

What key event happened between 1850 and 1900?

In the year _____, _____

When did the Panhandle region get added to the territory? _____

Circle an event on the timeline that is symbolized on Oklahoma's flag.

I was in a production of *Oklahoma!* Perhaps you saw me? I was the *star.*

History Files!

You produce an episode for the TV show *History Files!*

Circle a **primary source** you can use to tell about Martin Luther King, Jr.

Look at each source. Write a **1** next to each primary source, and a **2** next to each secondary source.

- photograph
- journal of someone on the Oregon Trail
- painting of an event by someone who was there
- film of an event
- observer's drawing
- book about Gandhi
- movie about a famous writer
- painting based on an event in history

- Confederate dollar

- George Custer

- encyclopedia

A **primary source** is a record made by someone who saw or took part in an event. A **secondary source** is a record made by someone who was *not* there. You can use these primary sources to tell about your family: a photo, souvenir, recipe, journal, or letter.

Create a primary source. Ask a relative about his or her life. Write four questions. Then ask him or her to write the answers.

Interview with:

Question 1:

Answer:

Question 2:

Answer:

Question 3:

Answer:

Question 4:

Answer:

Think of questions only your relative can answer about him- or herself. For example, *What is your favorite childhood memory? What kind of games did you play? What was school like? Who were your childhood heroes?*

FREE to be Me!

The kids at Paul Revere Academy write a play about American Independence. But the pages of the script get mixed-up!

| 1773 | 1776 | 1783 | 1789 |

Put the scenes in order.
Write the scene number and the year of the event.

Scene ☐:
The year is _____.

The colonies' leaders meet in Philadelphia. They list reasons they want independence from Britain. They write the reasons in the Declaration of Independence. It also states that all people have a right to "Life, Liberty, and the pursuit of Happiness." The colonists cheer!

Scene ☐:
The year is _____.

The war ends, but life does not get much better. The leaders realize that they also need new laws. One new law is that the people will choose a president. They write the new laws in the Constitution.

Scene ☐:
The year is _____.

The colonies belong to Britain. So Britain taxes their tea. *Now it's too expensive!* Colonists start a fight with British soldiers. They dump British tea into Boston Harbor.

Scene ☐:
The year is _____.

The colonies finally win the fight for independence. They no longer belong to Britain.

John Hancock signed the declaration. He wrote his name *really* big. That's why *John Hancock* now means a person's written name, or signature.

FACT or Fiction

You are elected president of the Davy Crockett fan club.
Now, it is your job to separate fact from fiction.

Davy Crockett and the Frozen Dawn

Davy Crockett was a smart and brave American who lived a long time ago. When he was only three years old, he saved his family by wrestling a bear to the ground.

Davy Crockett did so many brave things in his life that he was elected to Congress.

Davy was smart, too. One winter, it was so cold that the dawn froze solid. The ice made Earth stop spinning. Davy figured out how to melt the ice and make Earth spin again.

David Crockett: American Hero

David Crockett was an American legend and hero. He was born on August 17, 1786, in a small cabin near the mouth of Limestone Creek, in Tennessee.

Crockett only went to school for six months as a child. However, he served as a member of the Tennessee legislature from 1821 to 1824. He then served as a member of the United States Congress. Crockett died a hero's death in the Battle of the Alamo in 1836.

Circle the reading that is fiction.

What is a clue that tells it is fiction? _____

Underline the title of the reading that is fact.

What is a clue that tells it is fact? _____

Davy Crockett made up stories about himself.
He claimed to have killed 105 bears in one year!
Create a legend about yourself.

When I was ⬜ years old, I _____.

Whoa. Did you really do *that*?

BASIC Rights

A U.S. citizen has rights, or freedoms. The Bill of Rights names these freedoms.

freedom of speech	freedom of assembly	freedom of press	freedom of religion
You can say good or bad things about the government.	You can gather peacefully in a group.	You can write, read, and watch what you want.	You can practice any religion.

Look at each picture. **Name the right being exercised.**

Reading the news
freedom of _____

Civil Rights leader Barbara Jordan
freedom of _____

Gospel choir
freedom of _____

Child labor protest
freedom of _____

How do you exercise your rights? Write one way.

_____

_____

_____

_____

_____

_____

I wrote my opinion on bullying in our school paper.

I think we should have healthier food in the cafeteria. So I wrote a letter to the principal.

I moved here from Jordan with my family. We were happy to find a mosque in our community.

KEEP THE
PEACE!

George and Gina start a Peace Police squad.

They are always on duty. If there is a conflict, they can help.

In case of conflict:

1. **Walk away.**

   Wait until both people are ready to talk calmly.

2. **Smile about it.**

   It's easier to resolve a conflict if people are friendly.

3. **Compromise.**

   Each person gives up a little of what he or she wants.

4. **Ask for help.**

   Find a person to mediate (MEE-dee-ayte).

   This person can help settle the conflict.

- Think of a conflict you had or saw. How did it get resolved?

- Which steps are **easy** to follow?

- Which steps are **difficult** to follow? Why?

- Can you think of another idea to keep the peace?

When I argue with my cousin Gareth, he suggests that I count to 10 and eat an oyster chip. That's the problem! I can't count with my mouth full.

PEACE ON EARTH
WORK FOR PEACE

You join the Peace Police. Mediate each conflict.
Tell them what to do.

Crisis in the Cafeteria

Oliver and Ruby both want a banana.

Conflict: There is only one left!

_____

Basket Brawl

Zach and Danny want to play
basketball, but Ty has the ball.

Conflict: Ty wants to practice spinning.

_____

Poet vs. Yodeler

Dee is trying to write a poem.
Les and Jessie practice yodeling nearby.

Conflict: Dee asks them to yodel quietly, but they keep singing.

_____

Next time you have a conflict, smile.
See what happens!

Sweet Success

Sour Acres is a lemon grove run by the Rind family.
Mila wants to open a lemonade stand.
She buys 20 crates of lemons from the grove.

> The **producer** is
> _____
>
> The **consumer** is
> _____
>
> The **product** is
> _____

Mila opens the stand near a soccer field.
She sells over 200 glasses of lemonade
to thirsty fans and players. Now...

> The **producer** is
> _____
>
> The **consumer** is
> _____
>
> The **product** is
> _____

A **producer** makes a product or provides a service.
A **product** is a good that people grow or make.
A **consumer** buys a product or a service. An
entrepreneur (ahn-truh-pruh-NER) starts a business.

Mila makes a **budget** for her business.
This can help her make good decisions.

July Budget

Money Earned

Lemonade	$30
Strawberry lemonade	$14
Iced tea	$10

Money Spent

Lemons	$10
Strawberries	$6
Tea	$12
Sugar	$5
Cups	$5

How much money did Mila make in July? $ _____

How much money did Mila spend in July? $ _____

Did Mila make or lose money in July? She (made/lost) $ _____

In August, Mila will not sell iced tea. If everything else stays the same, how much money will she make in August? $ _____

Mila plans to buy a $30 electric juicer with earnings from July and August. How much will she have left? $ _____

Mila buys the juicer to grow her business. She can make more lemonade in less time.

With Rights,
RESPONSIBILITIES!

As citizens, we have responsibilities, or things we must do.
We do some things because it is the law.
We do other things because they are important.

| common good | volunteer | jury | consequence |

Complete each statement.

A _____ is a group of people. They decide whether someone has broken a law.

Getting a ticket or going to jail can be a _____ of breaking the law.

These kids _____ at a bicycle repair shop. They choose to work without getting paid. The repair shop then donates fixed bikes to kids who can't pay for them. This helps the

_____.

Voting is a **right** and a **responsibility**. People have the right to vote, and it is important.

People on the MOVE

Some people move, or *immigrate*, to a new country. They come for a job, education, or even to escape danger.

A group of Japanese women and Chinese men arrive at California's Angel Island, the "Ellis Island of the West." They bring their cultural traditions with them.

What are examples of Asian culture in your community? **Circle them.**

BIG BEN

Ben Franklin was one of America's founding fathers.
He was also a printer, a scientist, an inventor, and a **philanthropist**.

What Ben Franklin did:	How did it help people?
He set up the first library in the American colonies.	
He organized a fire department to help put out fires in Philadelphia.	
City streets were dark and dirty, so he set up a program to pave, clean, and light them.	
He raised money to build a city hospital.	

11-year old Olivia Bouler is a philanthropist, too! When she saw the Gulf oil spill on TV, she wanted to help injured birds. So she made drawings. She gave them to people who donated money to a rescue organization. She has raised over $200,000.

Olivia cares about: ____birds____

Her talent is: ____drawing____

What matters to you? What is your talent?

I care about: _____

My talent is: _____

Philanthropists give time or money to help make life better for others.

Answer Key

READING FOUNDATIONS

p. 8

(mistreat), (misjudge), (preview), (precook), (rebuild), (rework)

p. 9

unhappy ——→ not
reread ——→ again
coexist ——→ together
bicycles ——→ two

p. 10

Reheat, unkind, bicycle, misbehave

p. 11

Responses will vary, but may include:
dislike: to not like
imperfect: not perfect
inactive: not active
invisible: not visible
nonfiction: not fiction
nonliving: not alive

p. 12

nonstop; refill; unafraid; impatient

p. 13

(misuse, replay, unpack, bimonthly)
mister, ready, under, biscuit

p. 14

breakable, painless, powerful, windy, bravely, teacher

p. 15

comfortable ——→ able to give
dreamless ——→ without
skillful ——→ full of
painter ——→ one who does this
happiness ——→ the state of

p. 16

spreadable, adventurous, spoonful, gardener

p. 17

wind ——→ the movement of air
windy ——→ characterized by lots
          of wind
windless ——→ having no wind

teach ——→ to help people learn things
teacher ——→ someone who teaches
reteach ——→ teach again

name ——→ what people call someone or
          something
nameless ——→ having no name
misnamed ——→ given the wrong name

p. 18

careless, enjoyable, quickly, singer

p. 19

agree	grace	friend	sick	
x				-able
	x			-ful
	x	x		-less
		x	x	-ly
			x	-ness

p. 20

agin ——→ again
irth ——→ earth
litelee ——→ lightly
beecuz ——→ because
moove ——→ move

p. 21

Regular tunnel: blaze, slump, napkin
Irregular tunnel: friendly, straight, people

p. 22

de/ter/mine   ab/so/lute
un/til   his/tor/ic
de/mand   con/sist

SPELLING AND VOCABULARY

pp. 24–25

raegffi=giraffe   oynmek=monkey
latpeehn=elephant   oiln=lion
hteache=cheetah   sitroch=ostrich
azrbe=zebra   ilorgla=gorilla

pp. 26–27

scrambled eggs
crispy bacon
three buttermilk pancakes
orange juice

grilled chicken
mashed potatoes
green peas
skim milk

p. 28

Down   **Across**
1. dangerous   3. interesting
2. short   5. exit
4. narrow   6. down

p. 29

silent/quiet
inexpensive/cheap
applaud/clap
filthy/dirty
jump/leap
intelligent/smart

p. 30

crowd, cloud, queen, lawn, chalk, squeeze

p. 31

scram (first row)
scrape (second row)
scream (third row)
scratch (fourth row)
scrub (fifth row)

p. 32

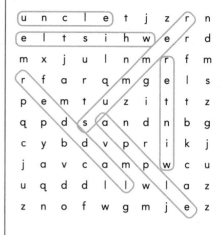

p. 33

(pillow, happen, lesson, sudden, letter)
design, chappter, incclude

p. 34

Today   dream
noise   real
trail   told
gold

p. 35

Stories will vary but the child should use:
magic carpet, hat, dog, money, donut.

p. 36

stare, gobble, warm, elated
Answers will vary.

p. 37

Rough, caught, thought, laugh, tough, brought, daughter
Laugh, rough, and tough should go into the trough.

pp. 38–39

They are a dime a dozen. ——→ They are not very special.
That will be a piece of cake. ——→ That will be easy.
It's a toss-up. ——→ It could go either way.
We're all in the same boat. ——→ We all have the same problem.
It's raining cats and dogs. = It is raining hard.
You are the apple of my eye. = You are important to me.
Actions speak louder than words. = What you do is more important than what you say.

p. 40

invited   saving
changing   stared
tasted   joking

p. 41

cried, puppies, cities, tried, carried, parties
Circled: cities, puppies, parties
Boxed: cried, tried, carried

pp. 42–43

gliding=glide
wished=wish
softer=soft
hurried=hurry
understandable=understand
Answers will vary.

p. 44

beat / beet
hair / hare
flour / flower

p. 45

bat: ~~an area around a lake~~
park: ~~relating to your health~~
change: ~~feeling very happy~~
letter: ~~the top of a building~~

p. 46

haven't   he's
doesn't   there's
aren't   what's
couldn't   she's

GRAMMAR AND MECHANICS

p. 48

circled nouns: sky, family, table, dog, room, car
circled proper nouns: Sparky, White House, Central Park, Mrs. Jones, Banfield School, Eiffel Tower

pp. 50–51

suitcase: shirt, soap, comb, book
thought bubble: hope, friendship, strength, joy

pp. 52–53

two coats; two trays; four plates; three dresses; three rubies
three loaves; three mice; two knives; four oxen; two feet

p. 54

Past Tense: waited, started, baked
Present Tense: waits; starts, bakes
Future Tense: will wait, will start, will bake

p. 55

allow=allowed
cook=cooked
need=needed
like=liked
pretend=pretended
trade=traded

p. 56

Circle:
SUNDAY: saw
MONDAY: went
TUESDAY: did
WEDNESDAY: run
THURSDAY: gone
FRIDAY: seen
SATURDAY: done

p. 57

Circle: was, is, am, were, are
Chart answers:

	Present Tense	Past Tense
I	am	was
He, She, It	is	was
You	are	were
They	are	were
We	are	were

p. 58

A simple sentence tells one complete thought. → We went outside.
A compound sentence is made up of two simple sentences joined by *am, but, or,* or *so.* → We went outside, and we played in the rain.
A complex sentence is made up of an independent clause and a dependent clause. → Even though it was raining, we went outside.

p. 59

Sample responses:
She plays soccer.
Dan helped the teacher.
Responses will vary, but the child should add a verb to sentences and may include:
She read one book that week.
Tom threw the ball to Sally.
Mitch likes to read mysteries, and his favorite food is toast. OR Mitch likes to read mysteries. His favorite food is toast.
The store is open every day, and they sell candles and soap. OR The store is open every day. They sell candles and soap.

pp. 60–61

statement → You traveled a long way.
question → Are you from outer space?
command → Stay on Earth, please.
exclamation → You have a strong handshake!
Answers will vary.

are   want
hope   does
visit   return
join

p. 62

it → book
him → Joe
his → Logan
she, they, it

p. 63

Answers in blanks will vary.

me   I
I   I
me   me
I

Drawings and sentences will vary.

pp. 64–65

sister's   school's
Luke's   men's
babies'   chickens'
children's   Iowa's
flower's

I: circle mine; draw an X over I's
you: circle yours; draw an X over you's
he: circle his; draw an X over him
she: circle hers; draw an X over her
we: circle ours; draw an X over we's
they: circle theirs; draw an X over them's
it: circle its; draw an X over it's
Sentences will vary.

p. 66

your   you're
It's   its
they're   Their

p. 67

yesterday
slowly
safely
near
down

pp. 68–69

smaller
largest
more
most

p. 70

Mon.	St.
Tues.	
Wed.	Rd.
Thurs.	Nov.
Fri.	Dec.
Sat.	
Sun.	Ave.

p. 71

Eddie, Bart, and Ava went to the park.
We need to buy apples, bananas, and oranges at the store.
My dog likes to walk, sleep, and play.
The audience listened, laughed, and clapped during the play.

p. 72

The path goes around the lake.
The flowers will bloom in the summer.
We skied down the mountain.
The book belongs on that shelf.
My cousin lives in the city.
The children played on the monkey bars.
We will eat at noon.
I see a storm brewing in the distance.

READING

p. 74

Two of the following three sentences should be underlined.
He demanded that all in the village obey him.
Anyone who did not was punished terribly.
Only one person was not afraid of the chief.
The photo on the left should be circled.
Possible answers: mean, tough, strict

p. 75

The frogs outside were making too much noise.
Circle: "Kill all the frogs!"
Answers will vary.

p. 76

So the people killed all the frogs. or
They did not like what they had done.
The person on the right should be circled.
Possible answer: embarrassed

p. 77

or think and covered with bites
Drawings will vary.

p. 78

Responses will vary.

p. 79

Circle: ALL
angry

p. 80

all living things are linked.
Circle the third paragraph.

p. 81

Responses and drawings will vary.

p. 82

See you later, slowpoke!
Drawings will vary.

p. 83

loyal, helpful, clever
Answers will vary but may include that Roy will see Joyce as a runner, not his sister.

p. 84

Knows About It: Leslie, Joyce, Meg, Rita
Does Not Know About It: Roy
Leslie tells the track team about the plan so they can call Joyce SJ.
Answers will vary.

p. 85

fast
So Roy will think SJ is a fast runner.

p. 86

Check: Yes
"Who is this SJ?" he asked.
Possible answer: "I am sorry that I called you slowpoke," Roy said. "I will never call you that again!" he said.

p. 87

heating up the track ⟶ running fast
take us to the top ⟶ help us win
warming the bench ⟶ not running
Possible answer: "I will run, and winning the race will be a piece of cake!" Joyce said.

p. 88

[X] proud
Roy smiled.
Underline: Roy smiled.
Drawings will vary.

p. 89

Joyce's Problem: Her brother Roy calls her slowpoke.
First Step to Solving Problem: Leslie writes an article about Joyce saying that she is a fast runner, but says her name is SJ.
Second Step to Solving Problem: Joyce lead the team to a big win.
Solution: Roy realizes that Joyce is a fast runner, and says that he will no longer call her slowpoke.

	Living Things Are Linked	Sprinting Joyce
problem is solved		x
problem is not solved	x	
a character learns a lesson	x	x

p. 90

This is the story of one amazing inventor.
Drawings and responses will vary.

p. 91

Aleck wondered how sound traveled.
Aleck and his brothers made a machine that sounded like a baby crying.

p. 92

False
True
False
Possible answer: Aleck is smart and inventive.

p. 93

Answers will vary.
Aleck's mother Eliza Grace Bell was deaf, which inspired him to want to help people who could not hear well.

p. 94

3, 5, 4, 2, 1

p. 95

"Mr. Watson, come here."

p. 96

Answers and explanations will vary.

p. 97

Bicycle
Lets someone use their arms instead of their legs to move the wheels
Answers will vary.
Drawings will vary.

p. 98

Circle: shadow puppets
Southeast Asia
puppet, shadow

p. 99

smoothly
Sample definition: not moving in a
smooth way
Bumper cars should be circled.

p. 100

shadow puppet: made from paper,
attached to a stick
Bunraku puppet: as big as a person,
moves smoothly
hand puppet: can be made from socks,
as big as a person

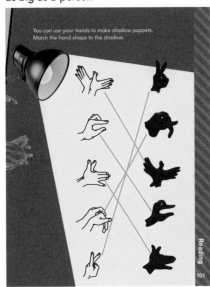

p. 102

That's because owls can see and hear
better at night.
Drawings will vary.

p. 103

The facial disc helps the owl hear better.
Kids should circle the light circle of
feathers around the owl's eyes.

p. 104

Owlets in a family may be different sizes.
Hungry owlets squeak!

p. 105

Owl facts will vary.

p. 106

green
Possible answers: fresh, warm
raining
excited

WRITING

p. 108

May include: bear, chair, snare, lair, hair,
wear, flair.
May include: boast, roast, most.
Responses will vary.

p. 109

Responses and poems will vary.

p. 110

hushed
toasted
rocky
damp
toasted
Star moon, underline bear

p. 111

Responses will vary.

p. 112

Option 3
Underline any two of the following: the
roar of the Mangy Monster; dropped
their toys; scurried into their house.

p. 113

budge   responded
whispered   crept
dashed   tiny
searching

p. 114

characters, setting, and problem
solve
solved
They thought a monster was after them!
They tried to hide in the basement.
They tried to hide in the living room.
They finally hid in the attic! They watched
until the monster hopped away.

p. 115

My brother got a new dog, and he named
it Missy. Every day, my brother feeds,
walks, and plays with Missy. He really loves
that dog!
All statements are true.

p. 116

Responses will vary. They should relate to
the picture.

p. 117

The story should include dialogue, a title,
and a picture.

pp. 118–119

Responses will vary.

p. 120–121

Answers will vary.

p. 122

1. Fill tub with warm water.
2. Gently put dog in tub.
3. Shampoo and rinse dog.
tub, water, shampoo

p. 123

How to Wash Your Dog
To wash your dog, you will need a **tub,
water,** and **shampoo.** After you gather
these supplies, the first step is to **fill the
tub with warm water.** Then, **gently put
dog in tub.** Make sure all of the dog's
fur is wet. Next, **shampoo and rinse
the dog.**
Drawings will vary.

p. 124

Answers will vary.

p. 125

How did the townspeople feel about Jack
at the end of the story?

p. 126

Circle: If you want to feel great and have
fun, I know how: Exercise!

p. 127

Color: 1, 2, 4
Number: 4, 2, 1

pp. 128–130

Responses will vary.

p. 131

Salamanders are amphibians,
like frogs.

Baby salamanders have gills.

Many North American salamanders do
not have lungs.

About 100 different kinds of salamanders
live in the United States.

The largest salamander can
grow up to two feet long.

Salamanders live in moist, dark places,
like under logs.

p. 132

Life cycle: Baby salamanders have gills;
Habitat: Salamanders live in moist, dark
places, like under logs;
Other facts: Answers will vary.

p. 133

Paragraph 1: correct spelling: "verry" to
"very"
correct grammar: "comes" to "come"
Paragraph 2: correct punctuation:
? to .
correct spelling: "aire" to "air"
Paragraph 3: correct grammar: "lives"
to "live"
correct capitalization: "smoky" to
"Smoky"
Paragraph 4: correct capitalization:
"united" to "United"
correct punctuation: . . . to .
Paragraph 5: correct grammar: "sees"
to "see"
correct capitalization: "next" to "Next"

p. 134

Check box: Salamanders are the most
endangered amphibian species in the U.S.

p. 135

Circle: principal; baby brother
Star: letter; informational paragraph
Box: persuade him or her to start a recycling program; tell him how to be a great baby brother

p. 136

Answers will vary.

MULTIPLICATION AND DIVISION

pp. 138–139

5 + 5 + 5 = 15
3 x 5 = 15
Each pizza should show 5 pieces of pepperoni.
4 + 4 + 4 + 4 + 4 = 20
4 x 5 = 20
2 + 2 + 2 + 2 + 2 + 2 = 12
2 x 6 = 12

pp. 140–141

There are 24 soldiers in all; 6 in each bin; 4 equal groups.
There are 5 planes in each bin; 15 ÷ 3 = 5
22 chips were in the bag!
There are 32 duckies in all; 8 in each bucket; 4 equal groups.
32 ÷ 4 = 8
There are 9 fish in all; 3 fish in each bucket; 3 equal groups.

pp. 142–143

2 pans of 8 nuggets is 16 nuggets
2 x 8 = 16 nuggets
4 x 4 = 16 nuggets
2 x 3 = 6 nuggets
4 x 9 = 36 nuggets
9 x 2 = 18 nuggets
7 x 4 = 28 nuggets
Reno found more nuggets!

pp. 144–145

Andrew has 20 coins in all.
4 x 5 = 20 coins
Marie has 10 coins in all.
2 x 5 = 10 coins
5 x 8 = 40 coins
7 x 5 = 35 coins
5 x 6 = 30 coins

p. 146

3 x 5 = 15 yards
3 x 5 = 15 yards

p. 147

Answers from top to bottom:
16, 2, 8; 32, 8, 4
48, 6, 8; 24, 8, 3
40, 8, 5; 64, 8, 8
72, 9, 8; 80, 10, 8

pp. 148–149

Bailey brushes Bo 10 times.
Bailey feeds Bo 5 x 3 times.
Draw 5 jumps of 3.
Bailey feeds Bo 15 times.
In all Bo has 4 x 6 toes.
Draw 4 jumps of 6.
Bo has 24 toes.
Bo entered 4 cats shows and got 3 ribbons in each. (Or vice versa!)

pp. 150–151

24/O, 24/O, 16/D, 36/T
Number line shows 8 x 2
42/I, 16/M, 50/E, 21/S
(GOOD TIMES!)

pp. 152–154

Shay opened the oven 3 times!
18 – 6 = 12; 12 – 6 = 6; 6 – 6 = 0
3, 3
8 – 4 = 4
4 – 4 = 0
2, 2

p. 155

In Ms. Wimple's class there are 4 equal groups of 5.
5 + 5 + 5 + 5 = 20
In Mr. Davis's class there are 5 equal groups of 4.
4 + 4 + 4 + 4 + 4 = 20
2 x 4 = 8
4 x 2 = 8
4 x 3 = 12
3 x 4 = 12
4 x 6 = 24
6 x 4 = 24

pp. 156–157

There are 6 groups of 2. 12 ÷ 2 = 6
There are 6 groups of 4. 24 ÷ 4 = 6
There are 2 groups of 7. 14 ÷ 7 = 2

pp. 158–159

It made 6 skips.
24 ÷ 4 = 6 skips
Carly's made 4 skips.
32 ÷ 8 = 4 skips
Zach's second throw made 8 skips down from 40.
40 ÷ 5 = 8 skips
Carly's made 7 skips down to 0.
28 ÷ 4 = 7 skips

pp. 160–161

Rosie: 4 rows.
Arden: 3 rows.
There are 5 squares in each row.
There are 4 rows of 5 in 20.
20 ÷ 4 = 5

pp. 162–163

5 x 4 = 20; 4
3 x 8 = 24; 8
z = 9; s = 7; r = 9; p = 4

p. 164

16 carrots   21 squash
24 beets   12 radishes
25 tomatoes   24 cabbages

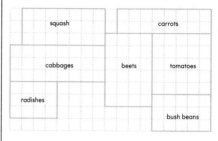

p. 165

1. 13/I   2. 29/T
3. 11/F   4. 10/E
5. 14/L   6. 29/T
7. 9/C   8. 21/R
9. 31/U   10. 15/M
11. 15/M   12. 35/Y
IT FELT CRUMMY

p. 166

0, 0; itself, 4; itself, 5; 1, 1; 0, 0; 0
10 x 1 = 10   0 ÷ 4 = 0
1 x 0 = 0   24 ÷ 1 = 24
45 ÷ 45 = 1

p. 167

6 rows of 4 = 24; 6 x 4 = 24;
24 ÷ 6 = 4
3 rows of 9 = 27; 3 x 9 =27; 27 ÷ 3 = 9
8 rows of 8 = 64; 8 x 8 = 64;
64 ÷ 8 = 8

p. 168

2	67	40	13	17	67	9
13	10	71	22	33	91	19
49	11	49	17	66	81	93
101	23	39	311	47	16	113
53	1	51	3	46	31	21
24	42	12	38	7	1	19

50
even

p. 169

9, 18, 27; 27
6, 12, 18, 24, 30; 30

pp. 170–171

Apples were gone in 4 days.
2, 2
6, 6
6
5

p. 172

30 ÷ 10 = 3
10 x 3 = 30
5 – 8 – 7   6 – 7 – 1
5 – 9 – 10   9 – 7 – 8

p. 173

2, 7, 14
6, 4, 24
3, 5, 15
14 + 24 + 15 = 53

p. 174

Number of Pitchers	1	2	3	4	5	6
Cans of pineapple juice	1	2	3	4	5	6
Bottles of ginger ale	1	2	3	4	5	6
Scoops of sherbet	6	12	18	24	30	36

6 cans of pineapple juice
6 bottles of ginger ale
36 scoops of sherbet
3 bottles of ginger ale
30 scoops

p. 175

5
16
24
7
LOST

pp. 176–177

24 eyeballs
There are 8 eyeballs in each jar; 24 ÷ 3 = 8
35 – 8 = 27
27 ÷ 3 = 9
25 + 5 = 30
30 ÷ 6 = 5
9 x 2 = 18
24 – 18 = 6

p. 178

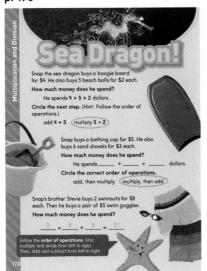

p. 180

about 100 eggs
40 + 35 = 75
25 + 100 =125
50 + 40 = 90
about 900 eggs
500 + 100 = 600
300 + 200 = 500
200 + 400 = 600

p. 181

about 25 left
40 – 10 = 30
90 – 60 = 30
70 – 30 = 40
about 200 left
500 – 200 = 300
800 – 400 = 400
400 – 100 = 300
about 150 chickens

pp. 182–183

200 + 10 + 5
two hundred fifteen
1000 + 300 + 1
one thousand, three hundred one
200 + 80 + 8
two hundred eighty-eight
6000 + 500 + 40
six thousand, five hundred forty
Answers will vary.

pp. 184–185

400 – 200 = 200 beads left, exactly 185

400, 414	100, 111	200, 208
200, 148	200, 197	400, 409
300, 273	0, 39	100, 104

pp. 186–187

700
200 + 40 + 2
500 + 30 + 6
700 + 70 + 8 = 778
900
400 + 60 + 9
400 + 10 + 3
800 + 70 + 12 = 882
900
300 + 80 + 5
500 + 10 + 9
800 + 90 + 14 = 904
800
500 + 20 + 7
200 + 60 + 6
700 + 80 + 13 = 793
800
400 + 90 + 5
200 + 50 + 4
600 + 140 + 9 = 749

p. 188

360, 400
400, 400
570, 600
950, 900
760, 800
140

p. 190

3, 12, 3

p. 191

1, 4, 4

1, 6, $\frac{1}{6}$

1, 2, $\frac{1}{2}$

pp. 192–193

3
2
6
9

pp. 194–195

12 dogs
24 guinea pigs
6 monkeys

p. 196

$\frac{0}{4}$, $\frac{1}{4}$, $\frac{2}{4}$, $\frac{3}{4}$; circle $\frac{2}{4}$

$\frac{0}{3}$, $\frac{1}{3}$, $\frac{2}{3}$; circle $\frac{1}{3}$

circle $\frac{3}{4}$

p. 197

Rocko
1/6, 1/6, 1/6, 1/6, 1/6
1/8, 1/8, 1/8, 1/8, 1/8, 1/8, 1/8
Lee

pp. 198–199

$\frac{2}{6} > \frac{1}{6}$

$\frac{2}{3} > \frac{2}{4}$

$\frac{2}{3} > \frac{2}{6}$

p. 200

2
16
8

MEASUREMENT AND DATA

pp. 202–203
40
11:25, 11:35; 30
1:30
12:30, 1:30; 12:30, 12:45

p. 204
4:16   5:50
6:22   9:51

p. 205
4:10 P.M. (small hand on 4, big hand on 2)
1:20 P.M. (small hand on 1, big hand on 4)
9:45 P.M. (small hand on 9, big hand on 9)
6:40 P.M. (small hand on 6, big hand on 8)

p. 206
bathtub: more than
nail polish: less than
milk bottle: about
vase: about
fish bowl: about
mug: less than
kiddie pool: more than

p. 207
circle: peanut, cherry, paper clip, gummy bear

pp. 208–209
7
5
11
Brain Toss
11
2
2
14
Hula Hoop: 8, 4-Legged Race: 12

pp. 210–211
Grade 3
25
90
Grade 5

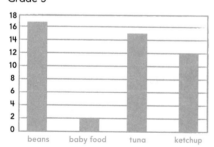

pp. 212–213
1
Blazing Bunnies
Terrible Twos, Squid Attack!
9
7
Picture graphs will vary.

pp. 214–215
9, 9
2, 2
14
9, 5
Animal Shelter
100
$100 / One hundred

p. 216
19
5
8
Cosmo!

p. 217

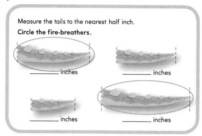

Measurements will vary.

pp. 218–219
3
6, 4
5, 13
Raft designs will vary.
19

pp. 220–221
(Answers can vary)
4, 2
12, 8, 20
Cowboy Rose, 2, 2; 2, 4; 4, 8, 12
Hibiscus, 2, 3; 4, 1; 6, 4, 10
Pink Phlox
Sunflower

pp. 222–223
16
20
14
16
28
Safe zone designs will vary.

pp. 224–226
1, 1, 1, 2
1 + 1 + 1 + 2 = 5
5 inches
1, 2, 2, 1; 6 inches
3, 2, 2; 7 inches
24 centimeters
10, 2, 2, 4, 8; 26 centimeters
15; 20 − 15 = 5
a = 5 centimeters
x = 9 centimeters
star = 15 inches

GEOMETRY

p. 228
impossible
possible
impossible
Drawing should be of a closed shape with 6 sides.

p. 229
1 right, 5 greater than right
2 less than right, 2 greater than right
4 right
5 greater than right
2 right, 4 greater than right

pp. 230–231
triangle   quadrilateral   pentagon
hexagon   octagon   decagon
row 1: parallel, perpendicular, perpendicular
row 2: parallel, parallel, perpendicular

pp. 232–233
Rhys, Skylar, Trixie, Hector

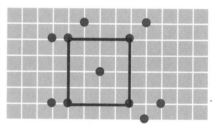

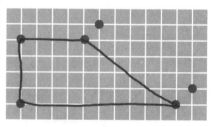

p. 234
A, F
C, E
A, C, E, F
B, D
C, E, F
A, D
B

NATURE OF SCIENCE

p. 236

weevil and butterfly: hand lens
amoeba and zooplankton: microscope
Drawings will vary.

p. 237

webbed feet ⟶ help it swim
hard shell ⟶ protects it
sharp toenails ⟶ help it dig

pp. 238–239

circle: tennis ball, duck, boat
It sinks!: penny, egg, rock
It floats!: bottle cap, ice cube, crayon

pp. 240–241

Answers will vary.

p. 242

Answers will vary.
climate
Draw a line from robin to temperate (green) region.
Draw a line from macaw to tropical (orange) region.

p. 243

back leg: 16 centimeters
front leg: 6 centimeters
difference: 10 centimeters
Sample answers: speed, mass

p. 244

80
Tuesday
Thursday
rain, umbrella
Tuesday, Thursday, Friday

p. 245

Answers will vary.
It is still too dangerous for humans to land on Mars. For one, the radiation is deadly! A Mars rover makes it possible to explore Mars safely.

pp. 246–247

3, 1, 2
Check each box.
Drawings will vary.

p. 247

Answers will vary.

p. 248

shoes, windows, coats, umbrellas, suitcases

LIFE SCIENCE

pp. 250–251

underline: seed, seedling, adult, fruit
Title: A Plant's Life
Stage: seed
Stage: seedling
The plant grows into an adult, which makes flowers.
The flowers fall off the plant, and the plant makes fruit. The fruit holds new seeds.

p. 252

Circle: ladybug on a flower, bee on flower.
Star: dandelion seeds, bluejay with filbert.

p. 253

Drawings will vary. Circle leaves.

p. 254

Circle: turtle, rabbit, rat, deer.

P. 255

cub ⟶ lion
pupa ⟶ ladybug
egg ⟶ chick
Drawings will vary.

pp. 256–257

1 to caterpillar
2 to eagle
3 to fish
4 to jack rabbit
5 to koala
6 to alligator
owl
Star: fish, caterpillar

p. 258

Answers will vary.

p. 259

cactus ⟶ desert
toucan ⟶ rainforest
mountain lion ⟶ mountain
blue whale ⟶ ocean
prairie dog ⟶ grassland

p. 260

a natural event, fast, destroyed, habitat, resources, nutrients, seeds, plants
Answers will vary.

EARTH AND SPACE SCIENCE

p. 262

Canyon
Valley
Sample answers: icy, rocky
Shoes on left should be circled.

p. 263

2, 1, 3
Erosion is on the left.

p. 264

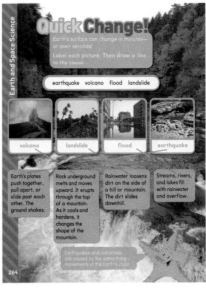

p. 265

10, 6, insignificant, far-reaching, 3

pp. 266–267

Answers will vary.

Resource	Renewable	Nonrenewable
Sun	x	
Oil		X
Natural gas		X
Wind	X	
Corn	X	
Water	X	
Diamond		X
Trees	X	
Coal		X

millions

p. 268

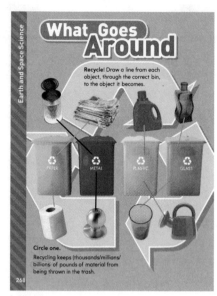

billions

p. 269

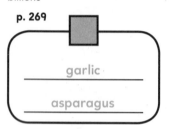

garlic

asparagus

blueberries

radishes

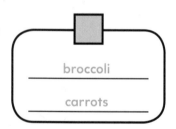

broccoli

carrots

pp. 270–271

condensation
condensation
evaporation
condensation

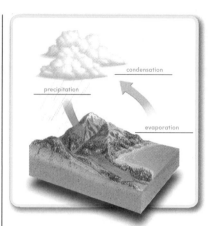

condensation
precipitation
evaporation

p. 272

low tide
The moon **cannot** be directly above this beach.
Sample answer: The tide pool will be underwater.

p. 273

weather	Texas
temperature	Kansas
blizzard	tree
tornado	car
hurricane	
cloud	

p. 274

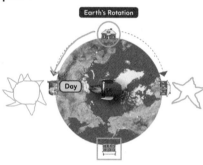

Earth's Rotation

Day

p. 275

new moon ⟶ crescent moon ⟶ first-quarter moon ⟶ waxing moon ⟶ full moon ⟶ waning moon ⟶ third-quarter moon ⟶ crescent moon

p. 276

aluminum, steel, copper

PHYSICAL SCIENCE

p. 278

soft, big, gray
Sample answers: yellow, wooden, prickly, shiny

p. 279

party hat ⟶ baseball ⟶ bread ⟶ pillow ⟶ milk ⟶ cat
Answers will vary.

pp. 280–281

C
C
P
C
P
C
Answers will vary.

p. 282–283

Lever: fork, rake
Pulley: climbing gear, crane
Wheel-and-axle: ferris wheel, pencil sharpener
Compound machine: ferris wheel

p. 284

1 cubic centimeter
3 x 3 x 3 = 27 cubic centimeters
27 cubes

COMMUNITIES

p. 286

forest, hills
bus driver, ambulance driver, shopkeeper
car, bus, clothes
Answers will vary.

p. 287

donating food	planting a tree
building a house	picking up trash

He volunteers for Habitat for Humanity, a group that builds homes for people who cannot pay for them.

pp. 288–289

building	dam
road*	bridge*
mine	tunnel*
canal*	farm

pp. 290–291

1. California	6. Kentucky
2. Florida	7. Delaware
3. Connecticut	8. South Dakota
4. Nebraska	9. Hawaii
5. Kansas	

Answers will vary.
California, Alaska, New York
Answers will vary.
cardinal
Answers will vary.

pp. 292–293

100 senators
Check each box.
Senate on left.
House on right.
Answers will vary.
1860

p. 294

Answers will vary.

p. 295

Make a dot after 1900.
Oklahoma becomes a state.
Circle the Panhandle.
1890, Congress establishes the Oklahoma Territory
and adds the Panhandle region.
1890.
1830 the five tribes begin to move
to Oklahoma

pp. 296–297

Circle 2. Martin Luther King, Jr.

1	1
1	1
1	2
1	
1	
2	
2	
2	

Answers will vary.

p. 298

2, 1776
4, 1789
1, 1773
3, 1783

p. 299

Davy Crockett and the Frozen Dawn
Possible clues: he wrestled a bear, Earth stopped
spinning
David Crockett: American Hero
Possible clues: he was born on August 17, 1786,
he was a member of Tennessee legislature
These are dates that can be checked.
Answers will vary.

pp. 300–301

press
religion
speech
assembly
Answers will vary.

pp. 302–303

Answers will vary.

pp. 304–305

Sour Acres, Mila, lemons
Mila, fans and players, lemonade
$54
$38
She made $16
$18
$4

p. 306

jury
consequence
volunteer
common good

p. 307

Answers will vary.

p. 308

gave people access to books
helped protect the city from fires
helped make the city cleaner and safer
gave people access to medicine
Answers will vary.

Inches

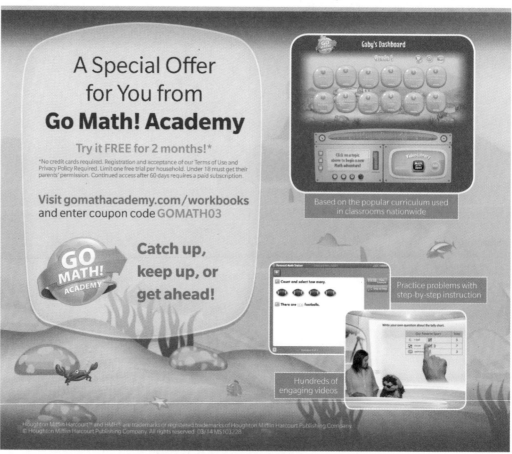